U0062880

中 央 美 术 学 院

设计学院 学生优秀作品集

中央美术学院设计学院学生优秀作品集·视觉传达

丛书策划　谭 平　颜新元

丛书主编　谭 平　颜新元

本册编著　航 海

编 委 会　吕品晶　江 黎　杭 海　谭 平

整体设计　谭 平

封面设计　孙 聪

版式设计　孙 聪

电脑制作　黄 悦　郝玉刚　高 凌

责任编辑　颜新元

责任校对　敖 群

出版发行　湖南美术出版社

地　　址　长沙市雨花区火焰开发区4片

经　　销　湖南省新华书店

制　　版　深圳利丰雅高电分制版有限公司

印　　刷　深圳彩帝印刷实业有限公司

开　　本　850×1168　1/16

印　　张　7.75

2002年1月第1版　2002年1月第1次印刷

印　　数　1－4000册

ISBN7-5356-1605-4/J·1517　定价：56.00元

3
目录
7
前言
视觉传达
8
广煜
18
庄春青
24
赵宇
36
刘宓
42
胡晓媛
52
王艳
62
罗凌霞
68
刘涛
74
陈礼
80
苏毅敏
86
陈曦
92
徐光东
98
王雪皎
108
梁远苇
116
吴笛笛

序

《中央美术学院设计学院学生优秀作品集》是设计专业成立六年来优秀学生作品的集中展示。其教学成果与特色所呈现的既不是一种模式或某种流派的表现，也不是以个别作品的优劣作标准的评价，而是诠释一种以创新的思想和开放的心态办学的教学理念。

面对转型期中国经济的迅猛发展所导致的社会需求的急剧变化，中央美术学院的设计教育为顺应社会发展的需要，在教学中将部分课程的设置向应用学科倾斜，这是符合客观规律之举措。然而，鼓励学生在校期间就积极投身经济主战场，抑或坚持教育之根本任务，引导学生以充足时间和精力去了解和掌握最本质最重要的思想知识和方法、探求人类最具普遍意义的和恒久价值的真理与学识，始终是我们关注与探究的问题。

人一旦置身于高速行驶的列车中便难以觉察到轨迹的偏离。教育同样需要不断地检测与修正发展的目的与方向。作为人文学科的设计艺术，在大学学习阶段尤为需要纯净的环境，需要与异化的现实社会保持距离。只有这样才能够使我们更清晰地认识社会、坚守真理；才能更清醒地洞察独特的思想所带来的潜在价值，而不只是注重实际的操作与迎合现实的妥协。学生是为思考和学会思考来到这里，我们的教学不仅有义务承传美术学院这一优良的教育思想，更有责任将其发扬、拓展，使之成为现代教育理念的坚实基础。

在历史发展的进程中，无论是一个国家、一个民族、一个社会都需要有一个能够超越功利的诱惑，具备批判精神和创新意识的团体，来自觉承担起人类文化传承和创造的伟大使命。

丛书所选择的学生作品，大多具有个性化、艺术化和实验性之特征，它充分体现了鼓励与培养学生独立思想的教育宗旨，我们力求使这块教学园地能够成为融会众多不同思想与观念的、教师和学生的教育与自我教育、独立思考的精神家园。

谭 平

中央美术学院设计系主任 教授

前　言

学生的作品最能体现一所学院的教学思想与特点。看过许多院校的学生作品集，其中多数都采取课程分类的方式来展示学生的作品，透过有所选择的科目的排列，我们可以感受到一所学院的教学的基本框架，这诚然是一种成熟、有效的编排方式，但这种方式的主要目的是全面展现学院的教学面貌，这种对整体的强调不可避免地在各课程作业的取舍问题上采取折中的态度以求得表面上的平衡；另一个弊病是，虽然书中充满了学生的作品，但你却无法领略到任何一位学生的较为完整的个人风貌。这二点美中不足的瑕疵在我们看来却是难以接受的，于是我们换了一种方式，从本系众多的学生中挑选了二十位学生，这种挑选没有年级人数的比例的考虑，没有课程科目的平衡考虑，唯一的考量标准就是学生的个人天分与整体素质。每个学生的作品来源由各任科教师推荐与个人自选相结合，于是，这个作品集看上去不够系统，更谈不上全面，但“全面、系统”既代表着一种成熟、一种完善，其负面意义是发展的停滞、潜在可能的消失。另一方面，我们的设计教学远未到达写总结报告的时候，事实上我们希望这一时刻永远不会来临。

这个作品集并没有试图汇集自设计系成立以来的所有的最好的学生作品，而只是挑选了二十名有特点的学生的不很完整的各科作品做专人介绍，这个看似随意的结集方式的背后有一个严肃的、诚挚的动机：我们希望这本作品集多一点人的体温，少一点浮华的修饰，因为在一个全面讲求包装的时代，人们更希望看到真实、鲜活的东西。

区区二十人的作品的汇集，只是阶段性的教学的产物，但透过它们，人们会感受到我们学生的心态、境遇与潜质，同时也必然地会体察出其中的不足与差错，正视错误一直是我们首选的教学态度，儿童心理学家告诉我们，对于儿童而言，出错往往发生在儿童不满现状、试图有所改变的时候，是好事情，这一创造性的描述非常适合我们这个建立不满 6 周年的年轻的设计系——它的教员和学生们。

杭　海

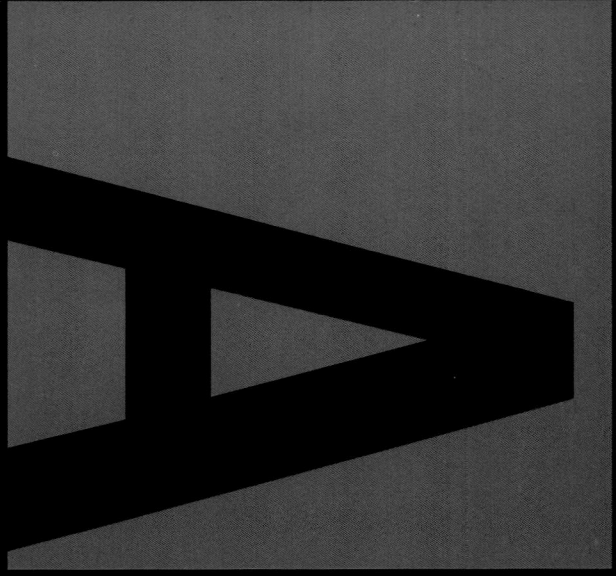

广煜

年出生于北京市

1994 年考入北京市工艺美术学校

1998 年考入中央美术学院设计系

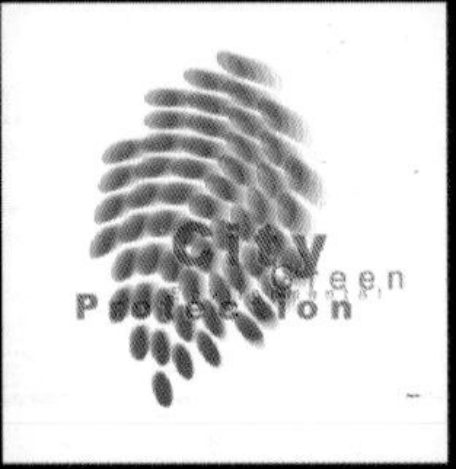
Grey
Green
Possession

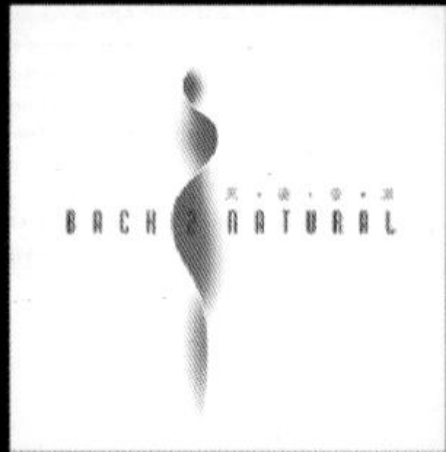
BACK
NATURAL

the sound of
the beautiful
T OG ETH

CD 包装设计

rad i oh ead

r adi o hea d

s i l e n t

a heart thats full up like a landfill, a job that slowly kills you
bruises that wont heal.

you look so tired-unhappy, bring down the movement, they don't
they don't speak for us. a hundred emotions conveying
and no words to express how we feel

i'll take a quiet life
no alarms
no surprises-no alarms
silent.

silent.

this is my final fit - my final
no alarms and no surprises. no
no alarms and no surprises please

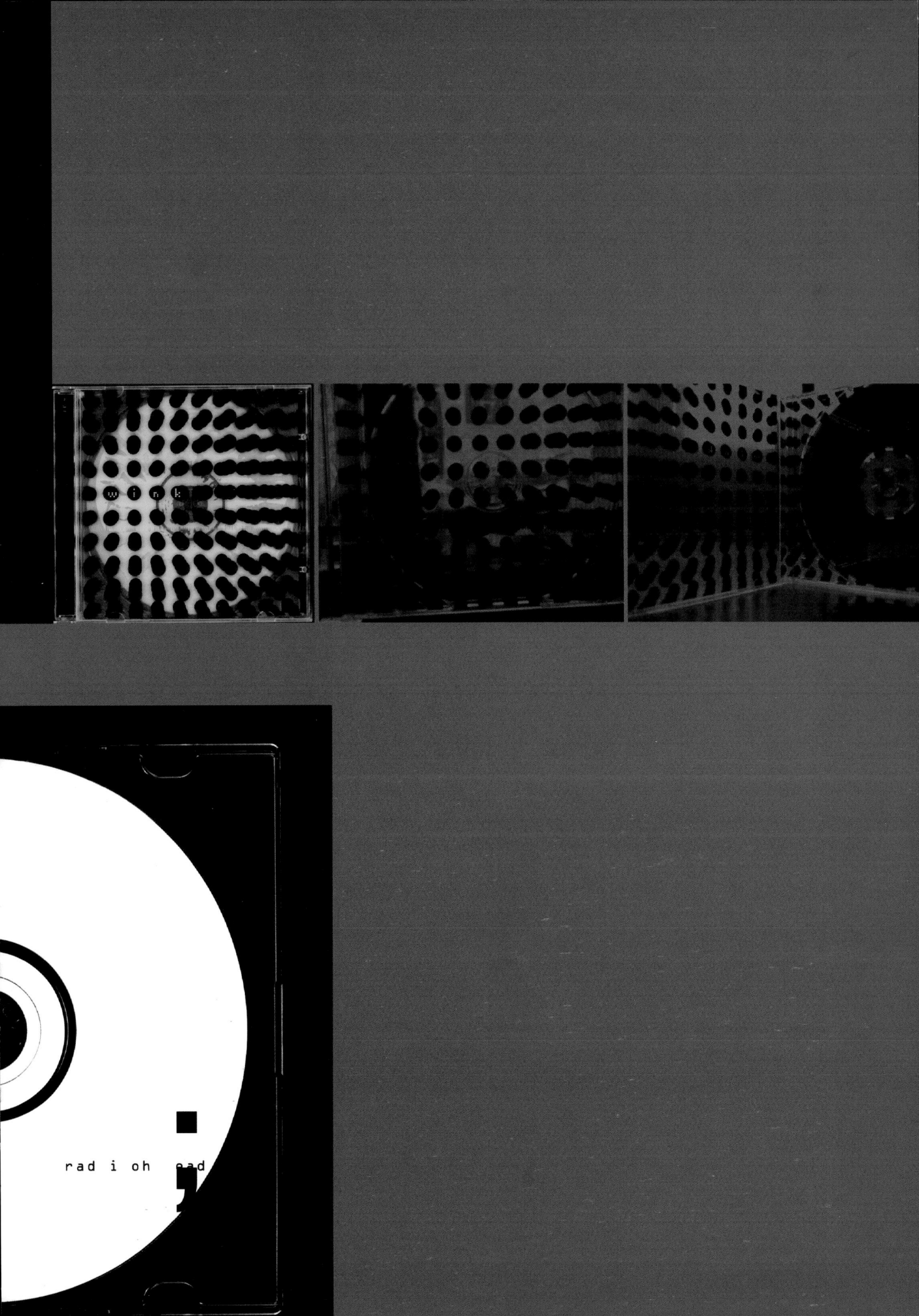
w i n k
rad i oh ead

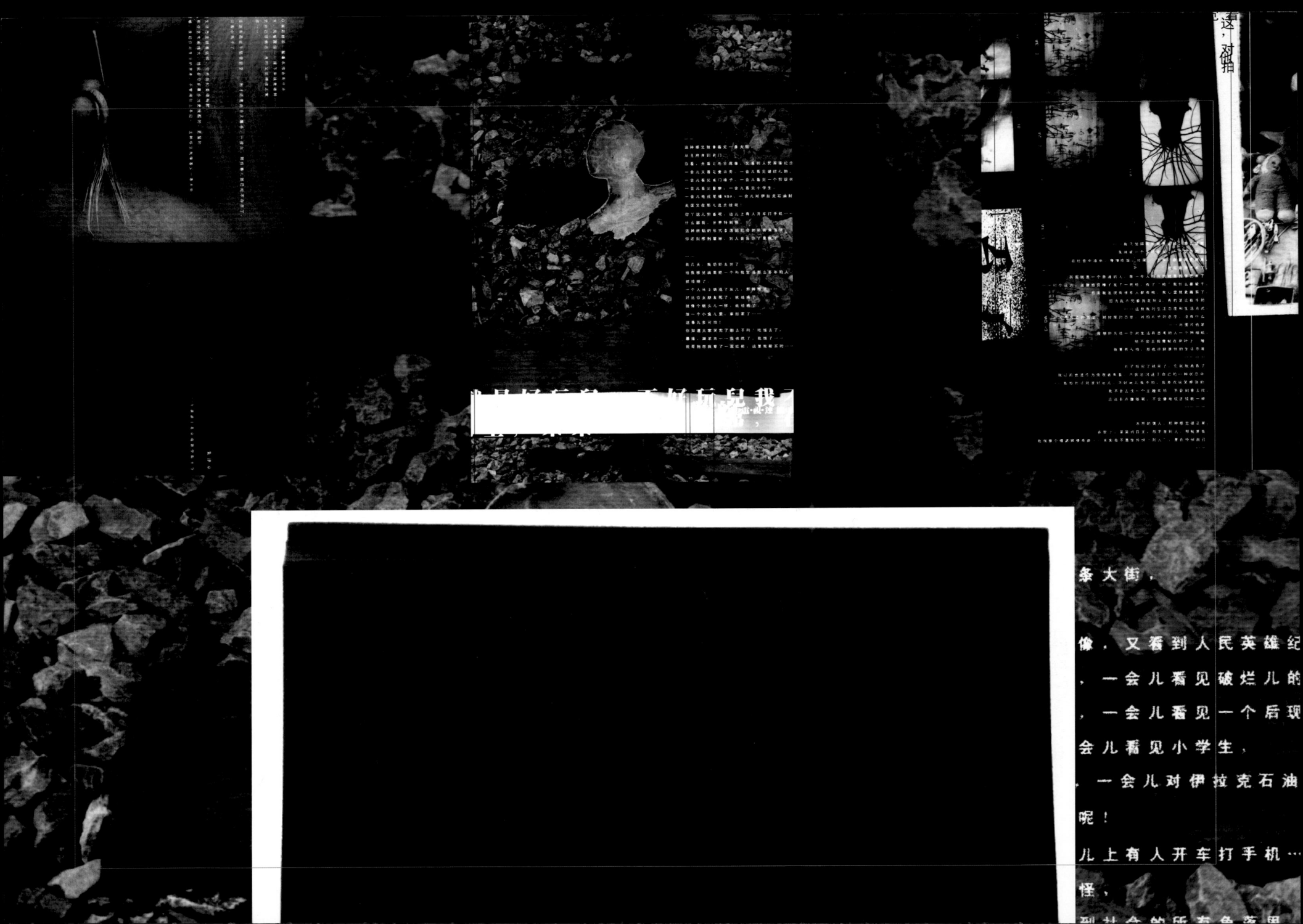

条大街，

像，又看到人民英雄纪

，一会儿看见破烂儿的

，一会儿看见一个后现

会儿看见小学生，

，一会儿对伊拉克石油

呢！

儿上有人开车打手机…

怪，

……

生活实际上是很混乱的，你要是直视它，能叫你精神分裂，

你必须学的麻木，你必须什么都接受，你才能有出路……

……

就得靠喝黄汤子生活，你要觉得黄汤子臭的话，你立刻就得死，

你必须抽自己大嘴巴

“这黄汤子真他妈香，我觉得象COCA COLA，我觉得象速溶咖啡”，……

……

当你领悟生活就是热热的一泡狗屎，

你就忍不住要拿一双新鞋往狗屎上踩……

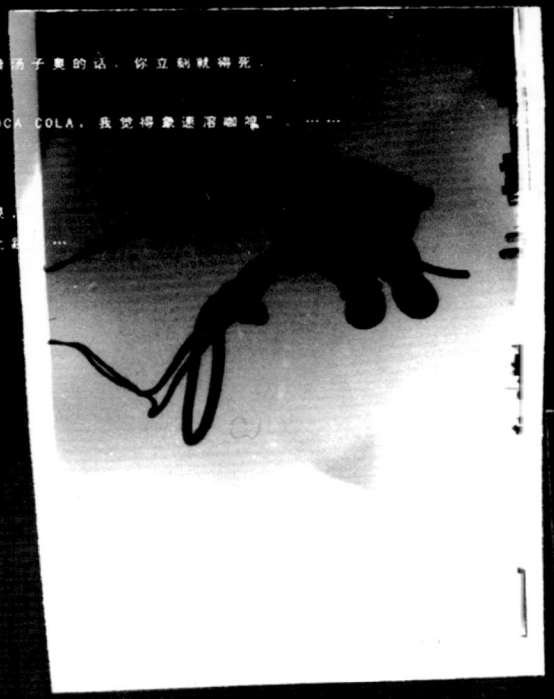

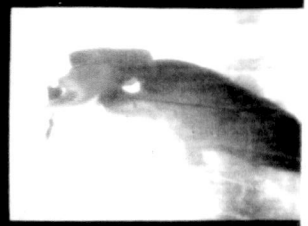

了，

和我生活那么多年的人

儿，那种感觉……

就给烧了，

就给烧了，

回家了……

去干吗？吃饭去了，

也吃了。我饿了……

红鞋，这是我新买的……

我

重·视·连

标题设计……

去，

来来

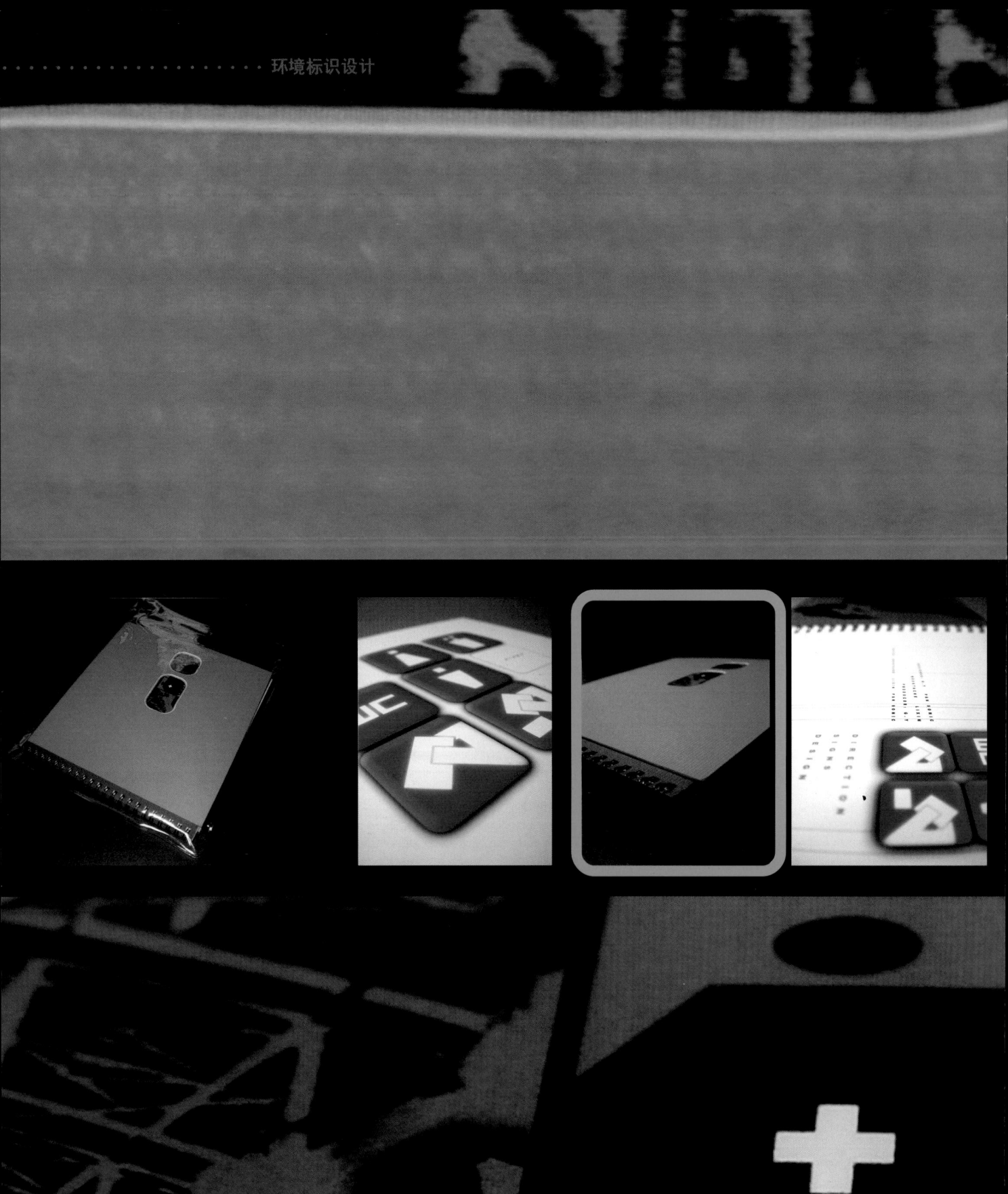

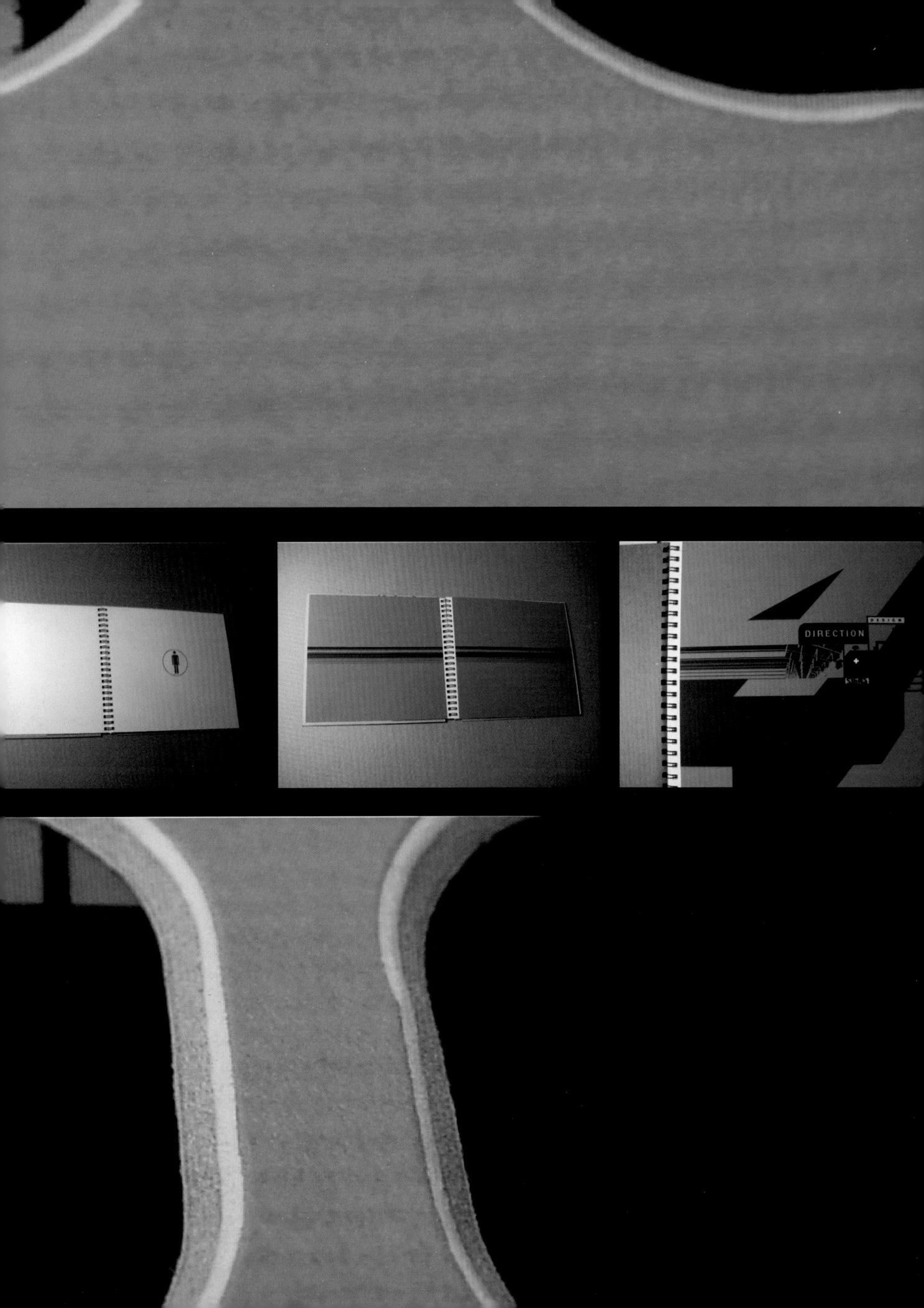
DIRECTION
DESIGN

3

庄春青

1977 年 2 月 18 日出生

1996 年毕业于中央美术学院设计系获学士学位

现为北京工艺美术学校平面部教师

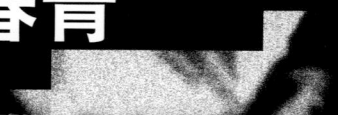

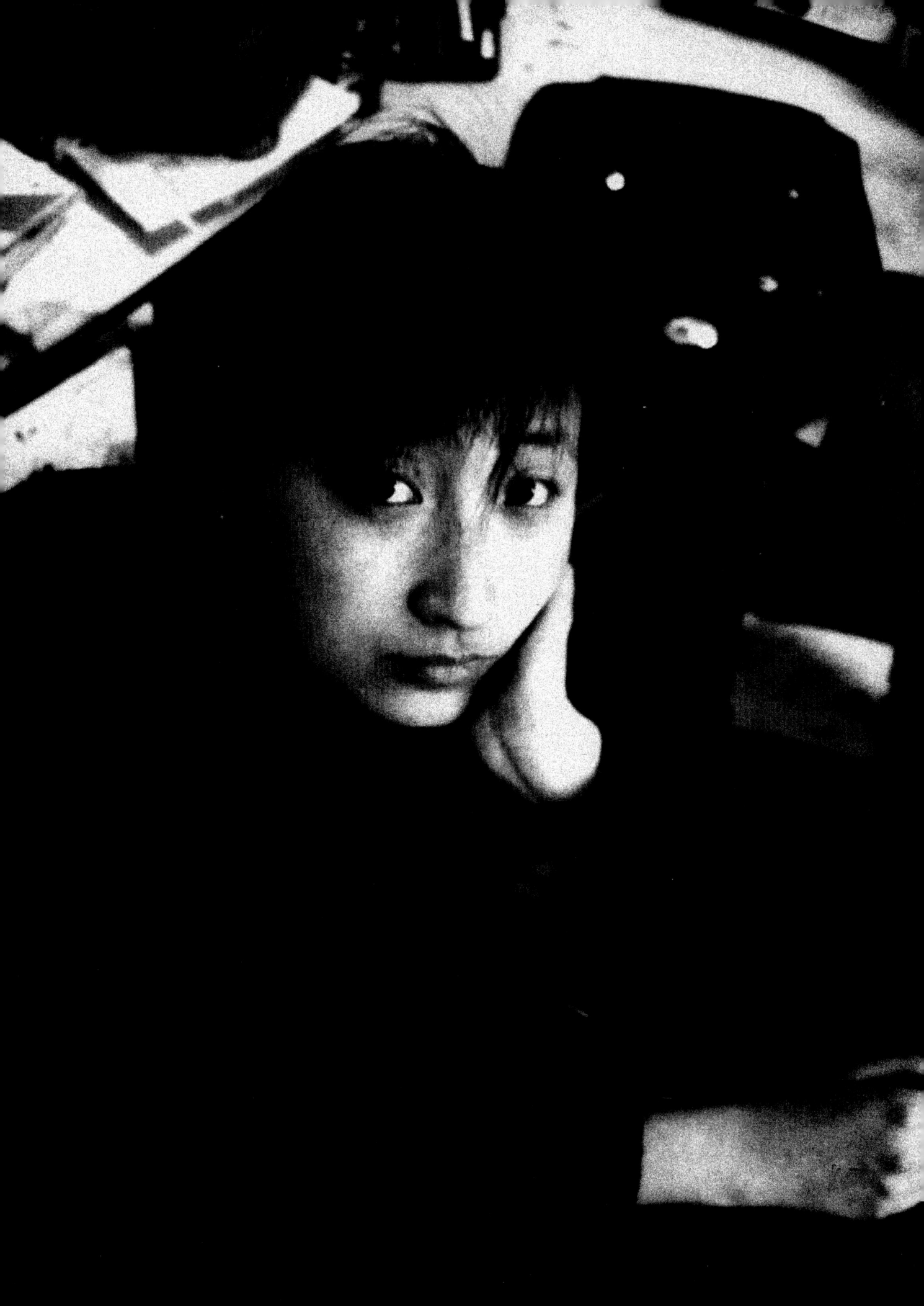

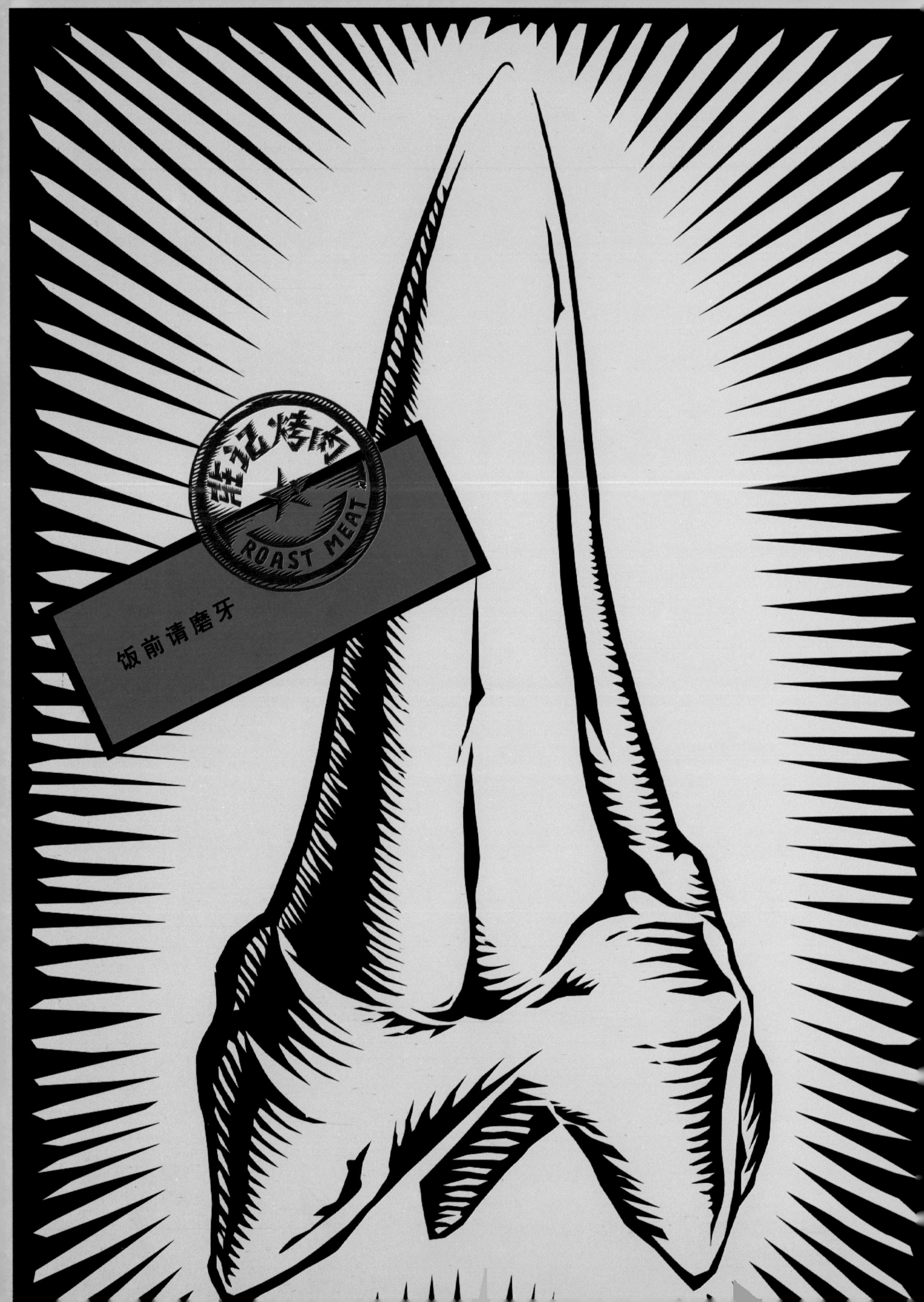
饭前请磨牙
ROAST MEAT

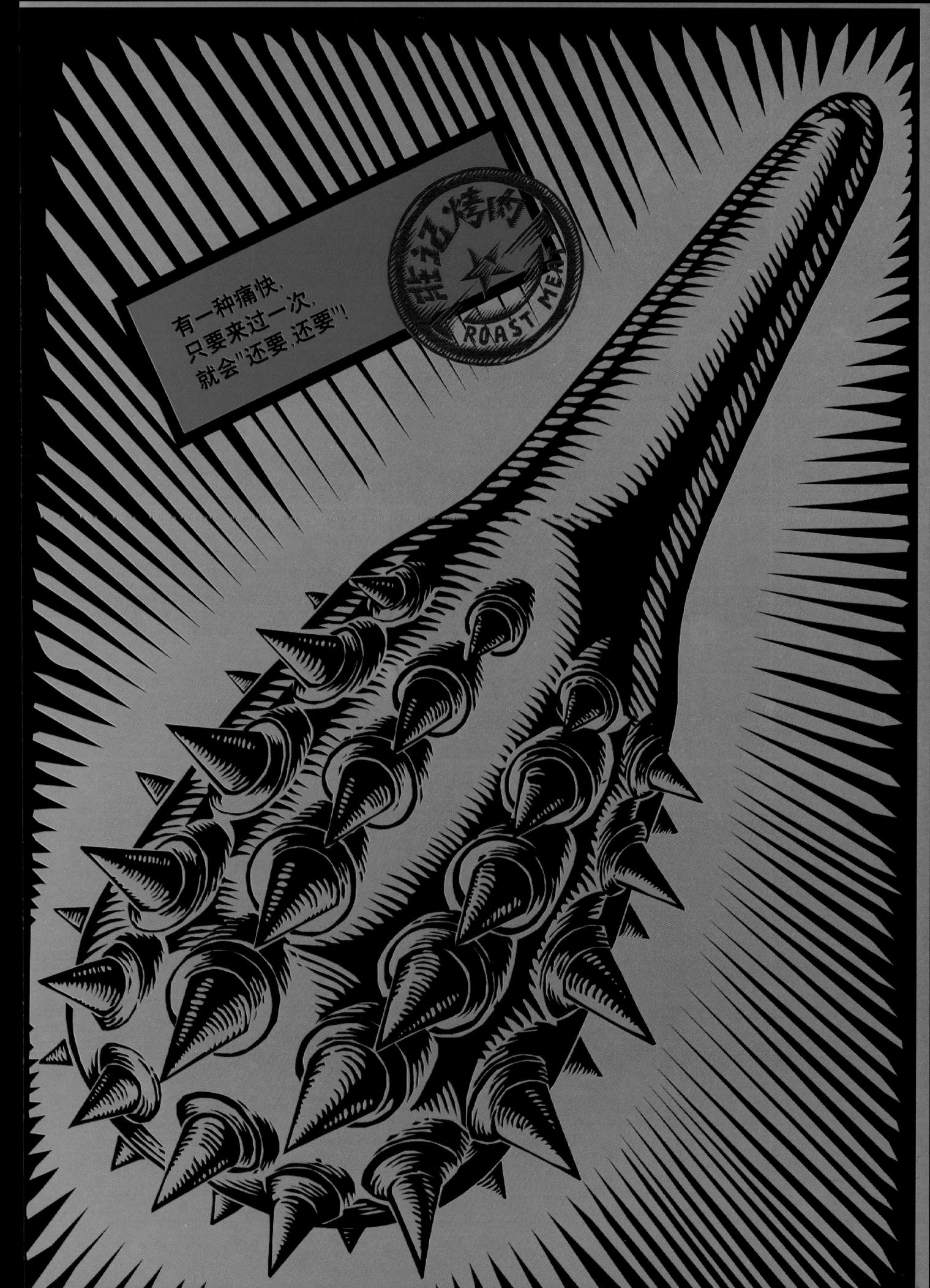
有一种痛快,
只要来过一次,
就会"还要,还要"!
ROAST MEAT

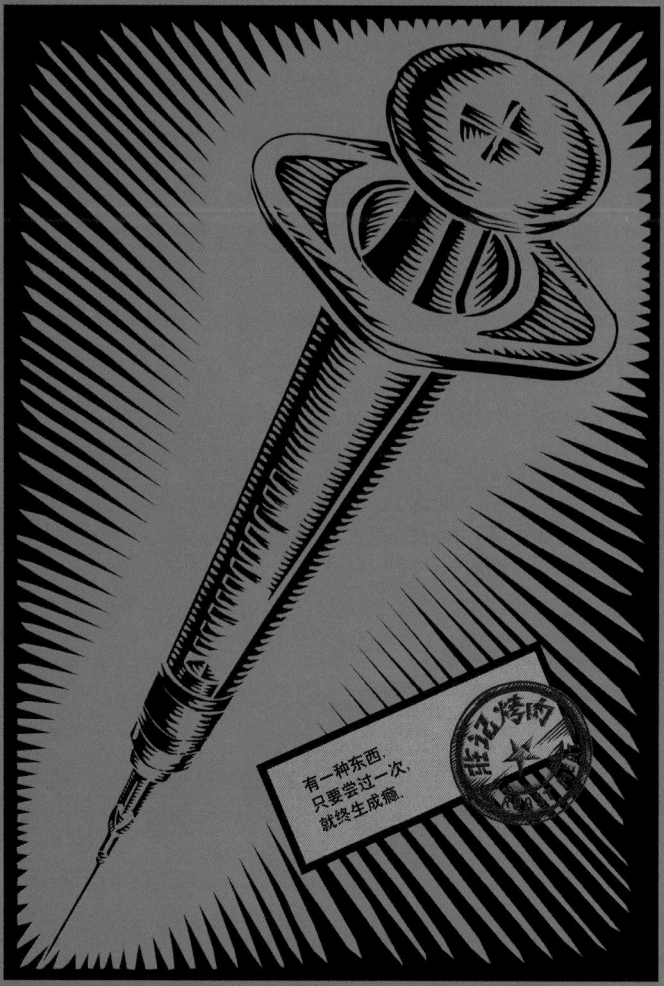
有一种东西，
只要尝过一次，
就终生成瘾。
非洲烤肉

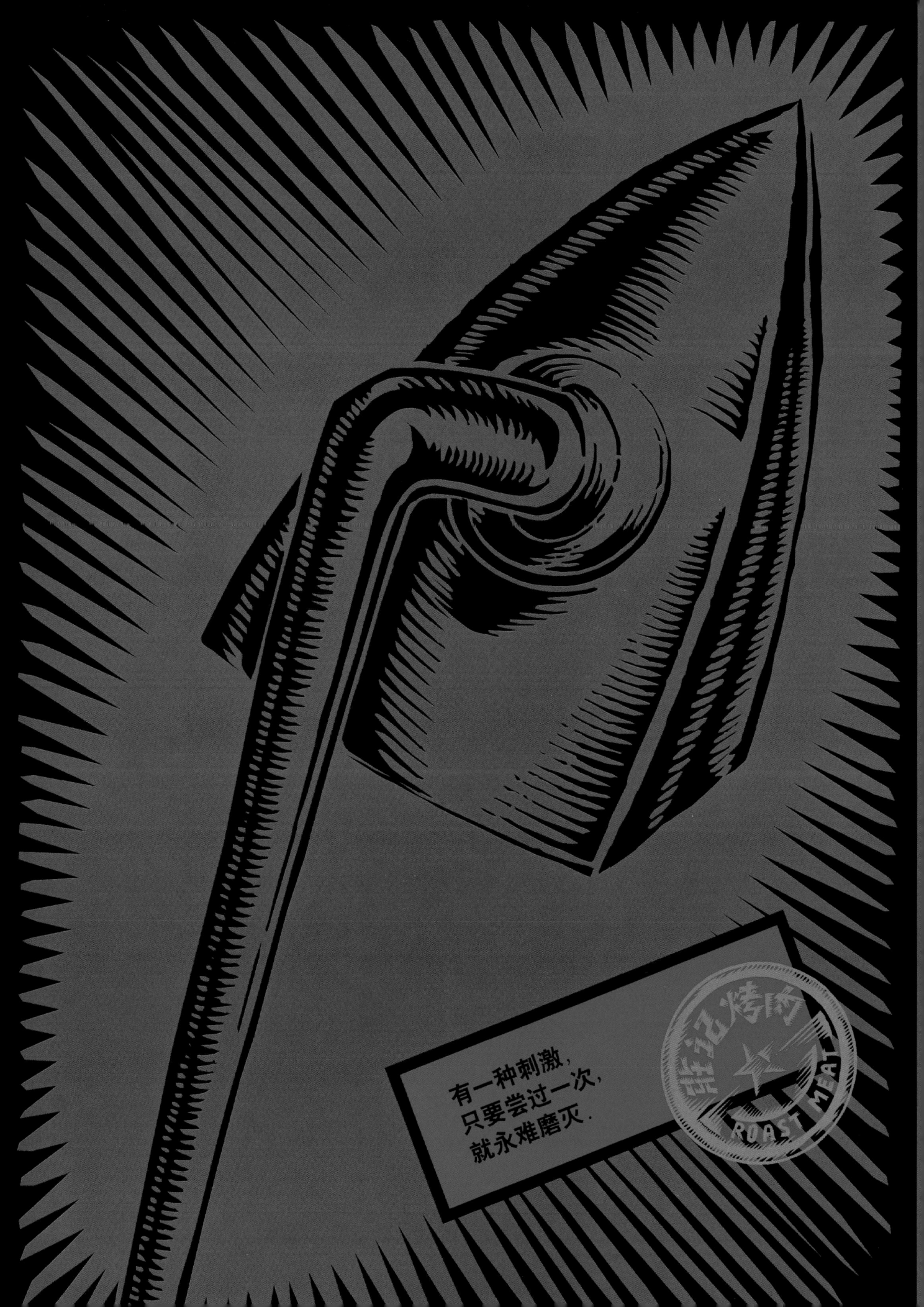
有一种刺激，
只要尝过一次，
就永难磨灭.
桂记烤肉
ROAST MEAT

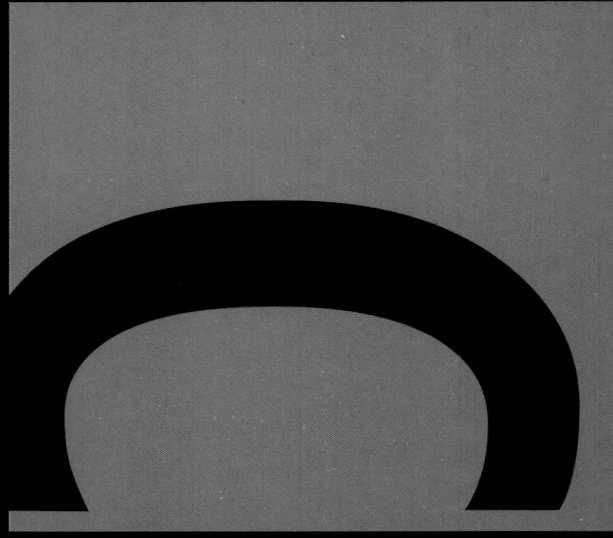

赵 宇

1979 年出生于河北省石家庄市

1994 年考入中央美术学院附中

1998 年考入中央美术学院设计系

2000 年作品《接进来》系列获“第九届台湾中国时报广告金 犢奖”入选奖。

作品《net+bar》获清华大学建筑学院 2000 年度“水晶石杯“学生建筑设计竞赛二等奖。

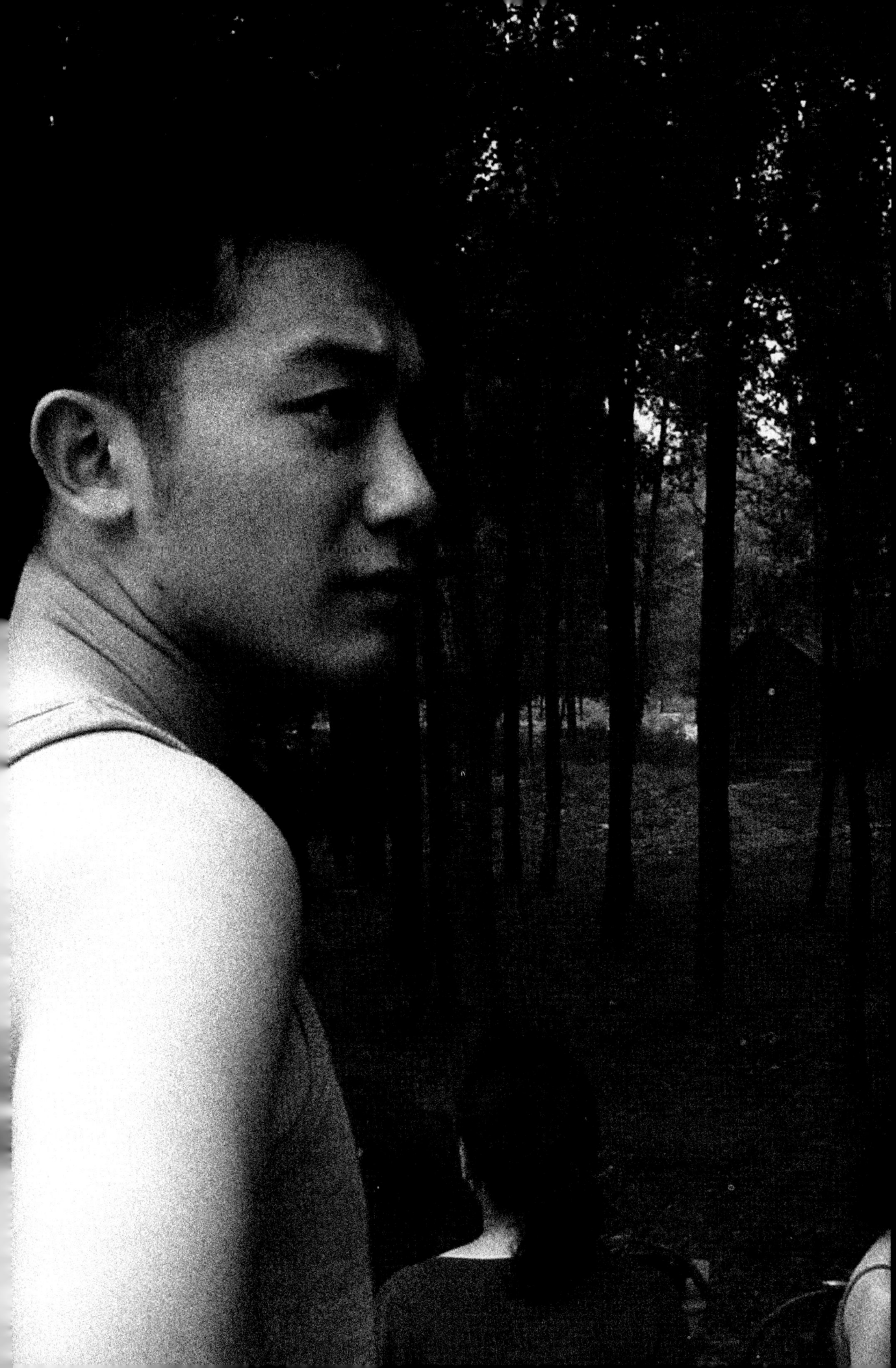

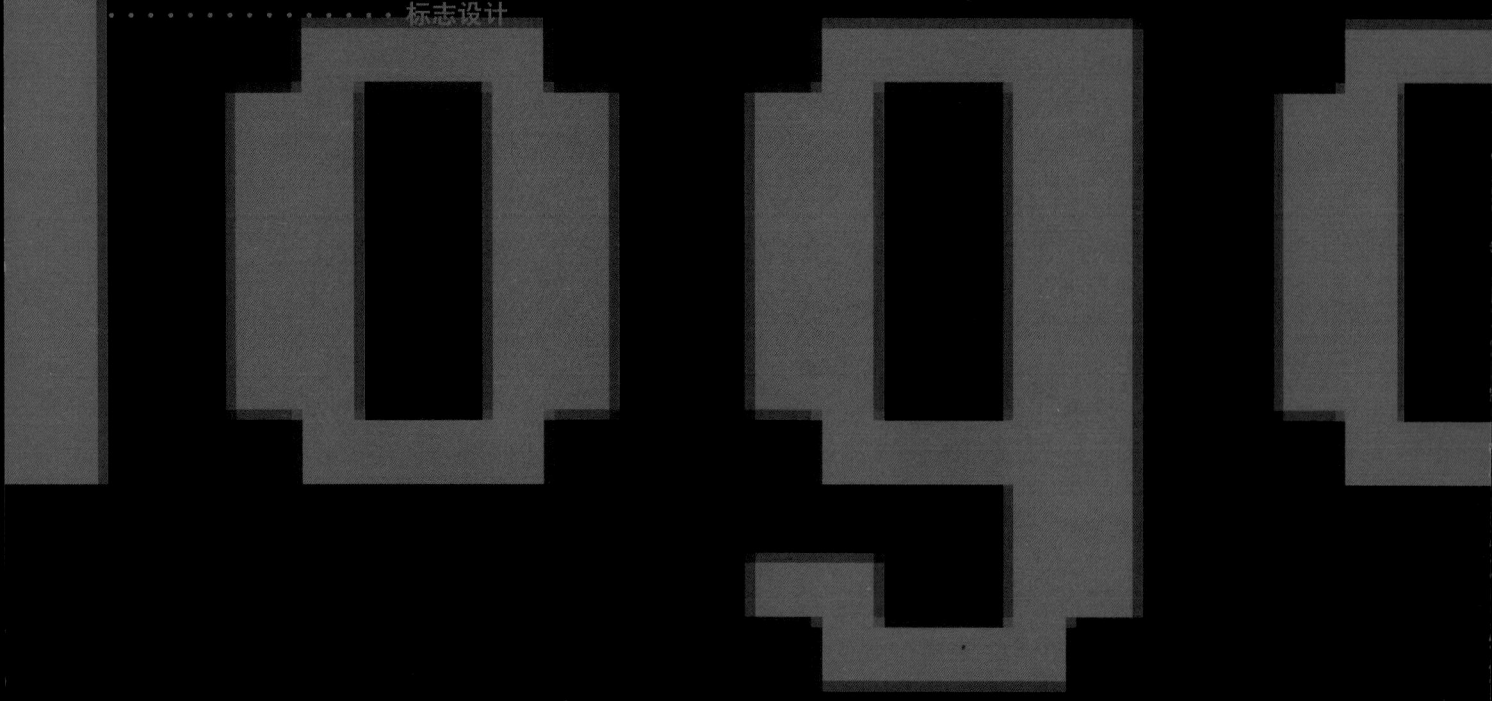
logo

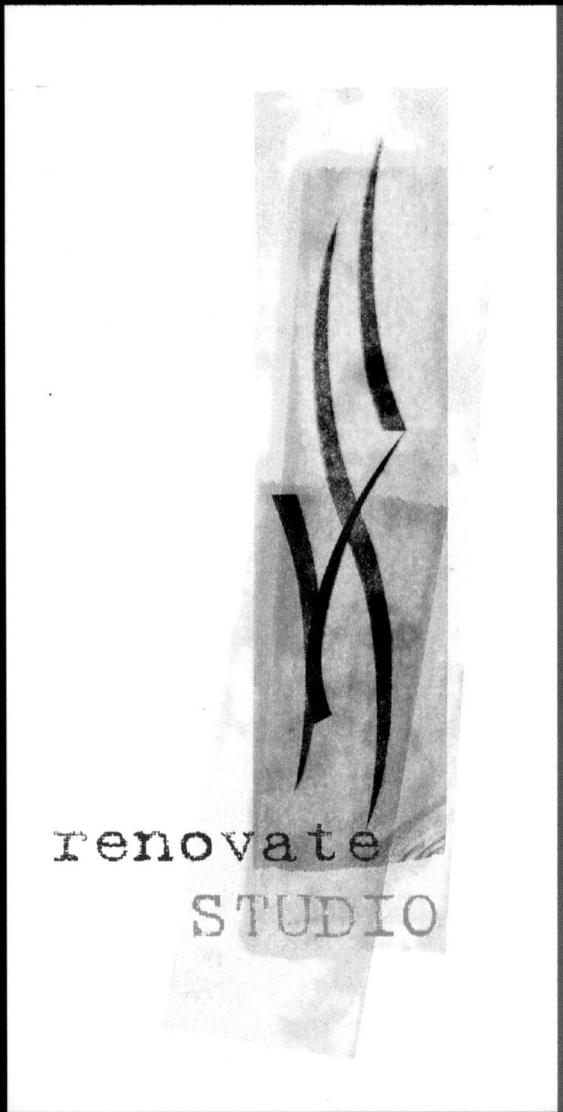
renovate
STUDIO

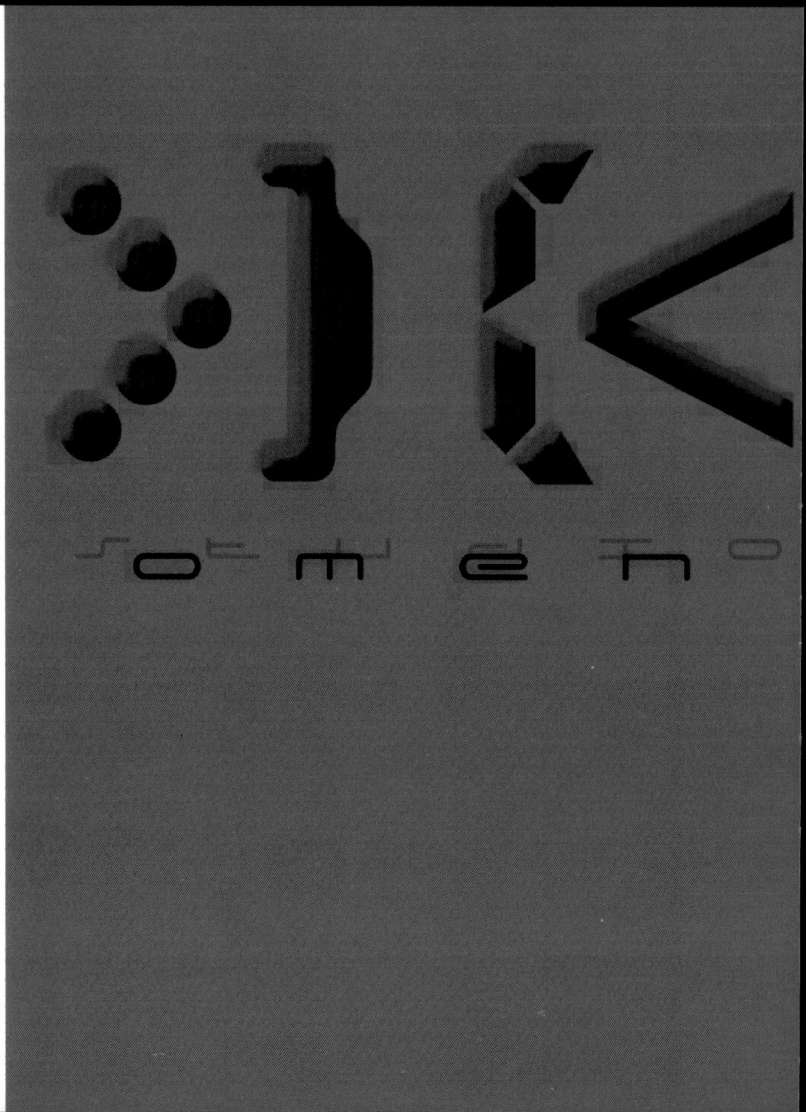
omen

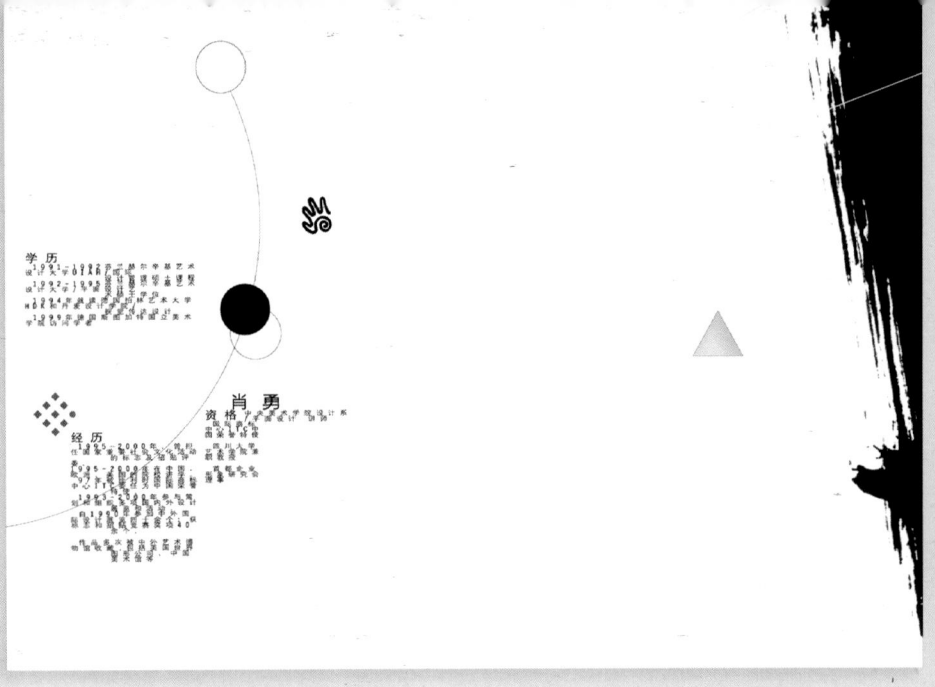
学 历
肖 勇
资 格
经 历

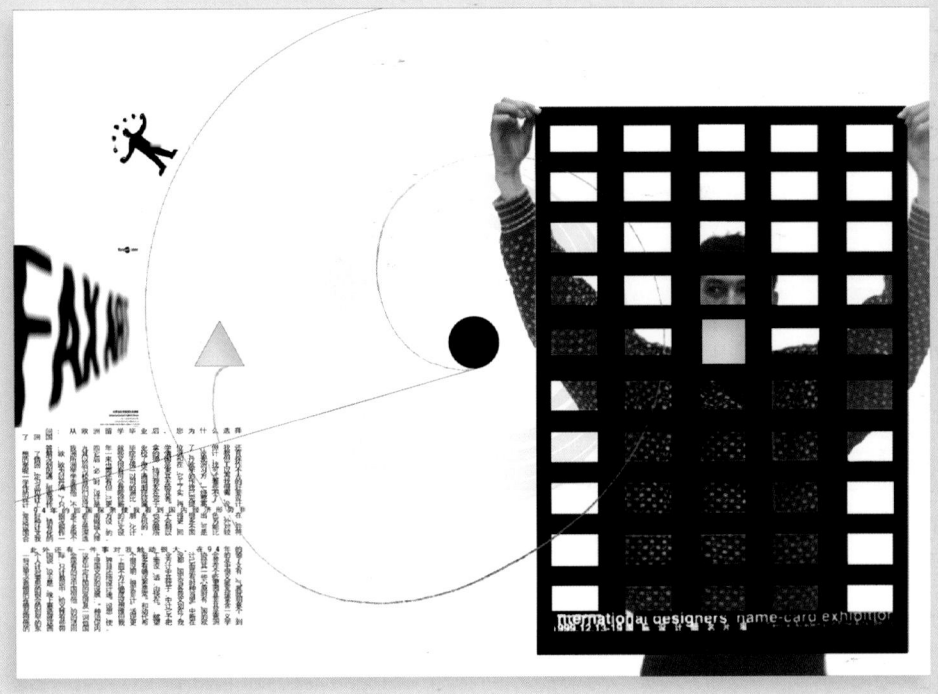
FAX

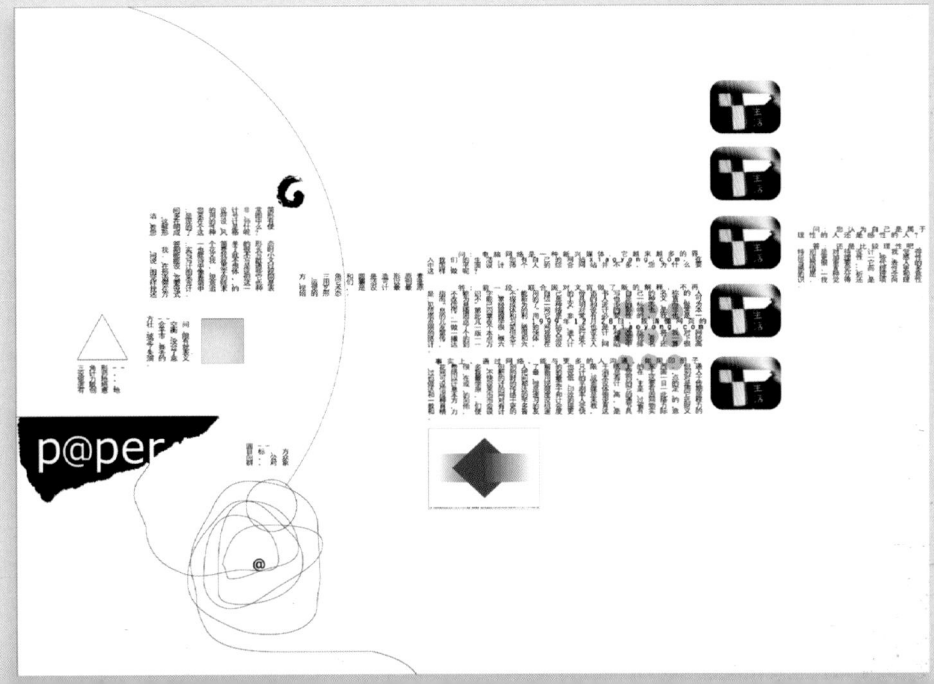
p@per

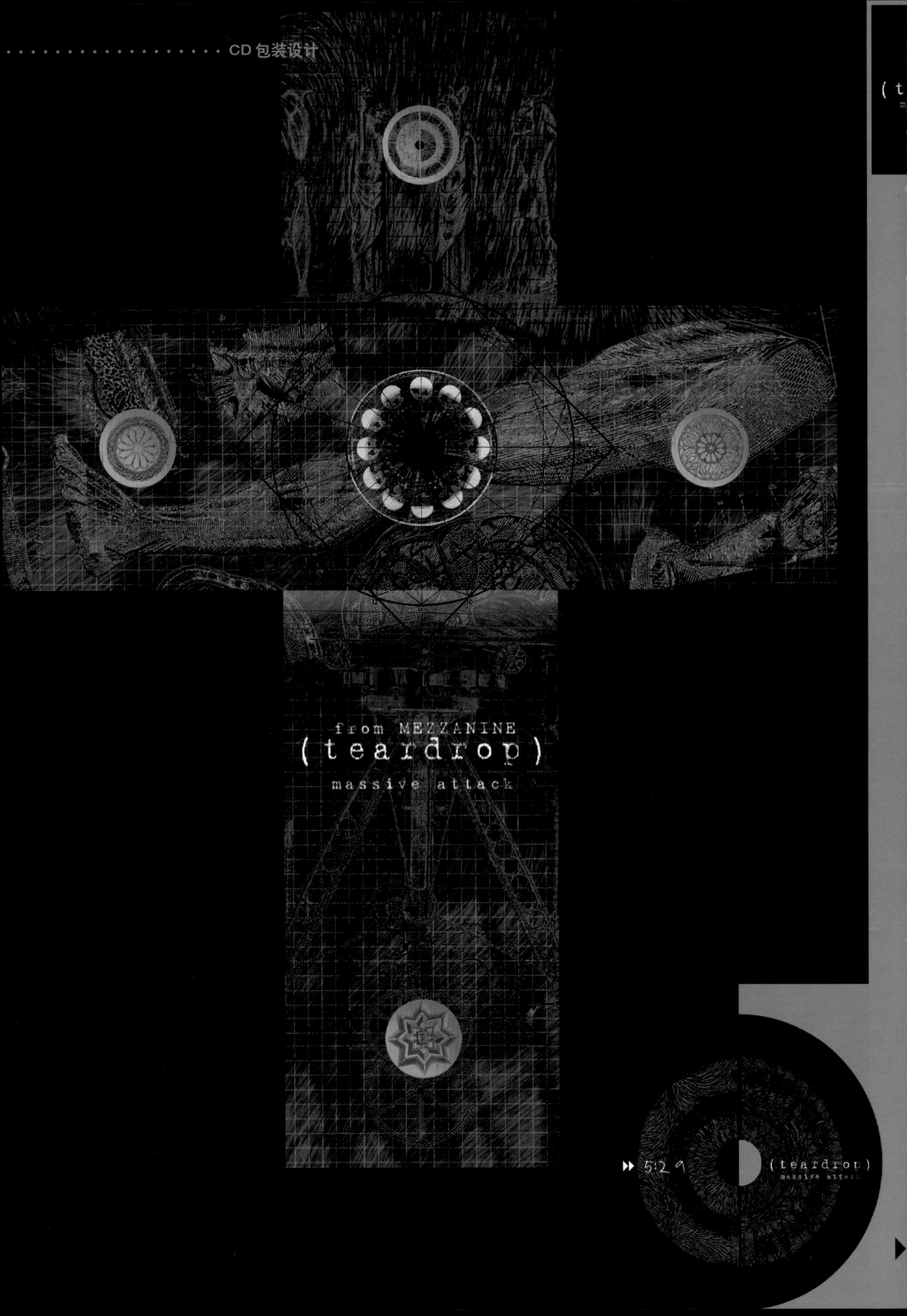
from MEZZANINE
(teardrop)
massive attack
5:29
(teardrop)

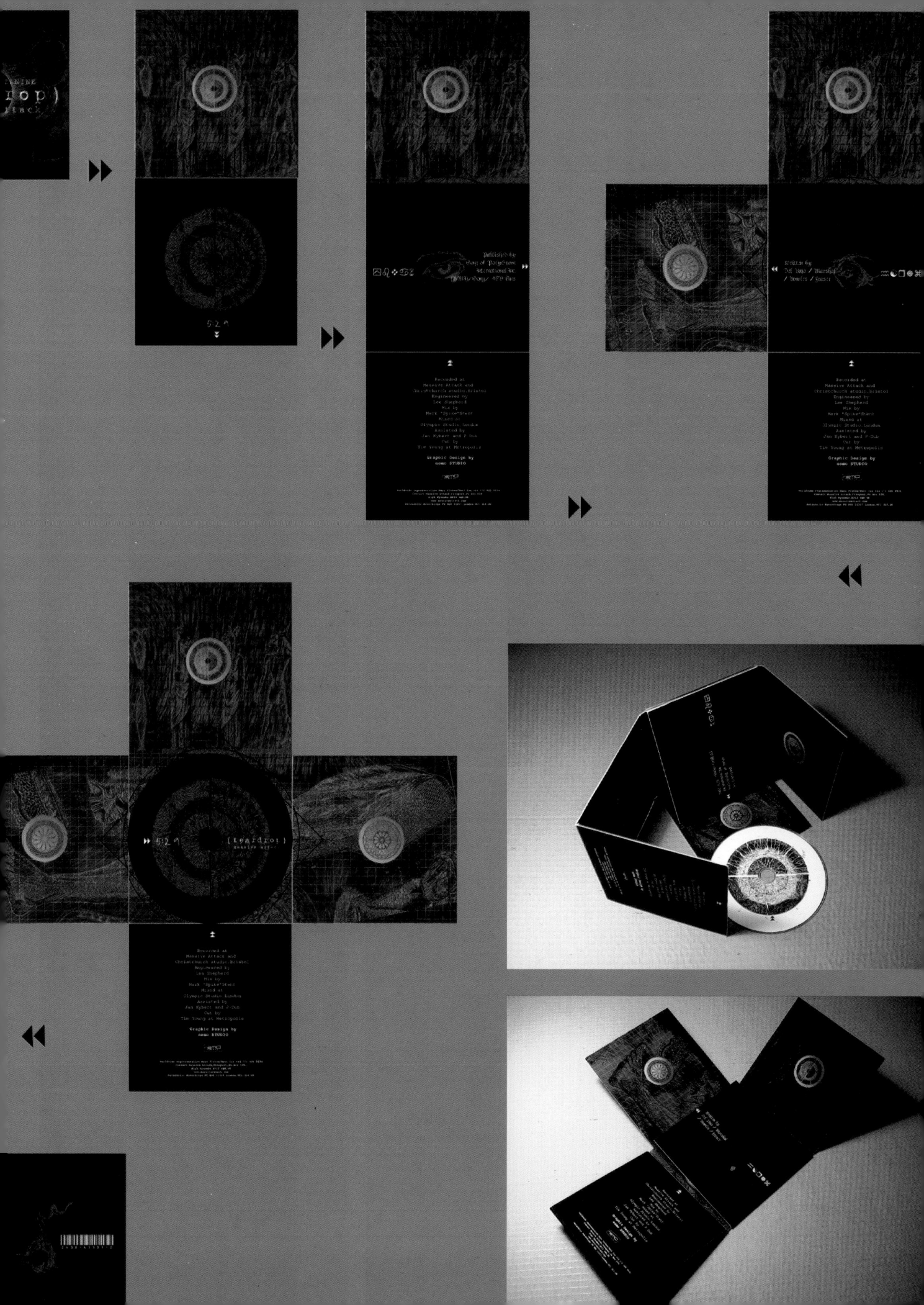
Recorded at
Massive Attack and
Christchurch studio,Bristol
Engineered by
Lee Shepherd
Mix by
Mark "Spike"Stent
Mixed at
Olympic Studio London
Assisted by
Jan Kybert and P-Dub
Cut by
Tim Young at Metropolis
Graphic Design by
nemo STUDIO
Written by
Del Naja / Marshal
/ Vowles / Grant
{leadfoot}

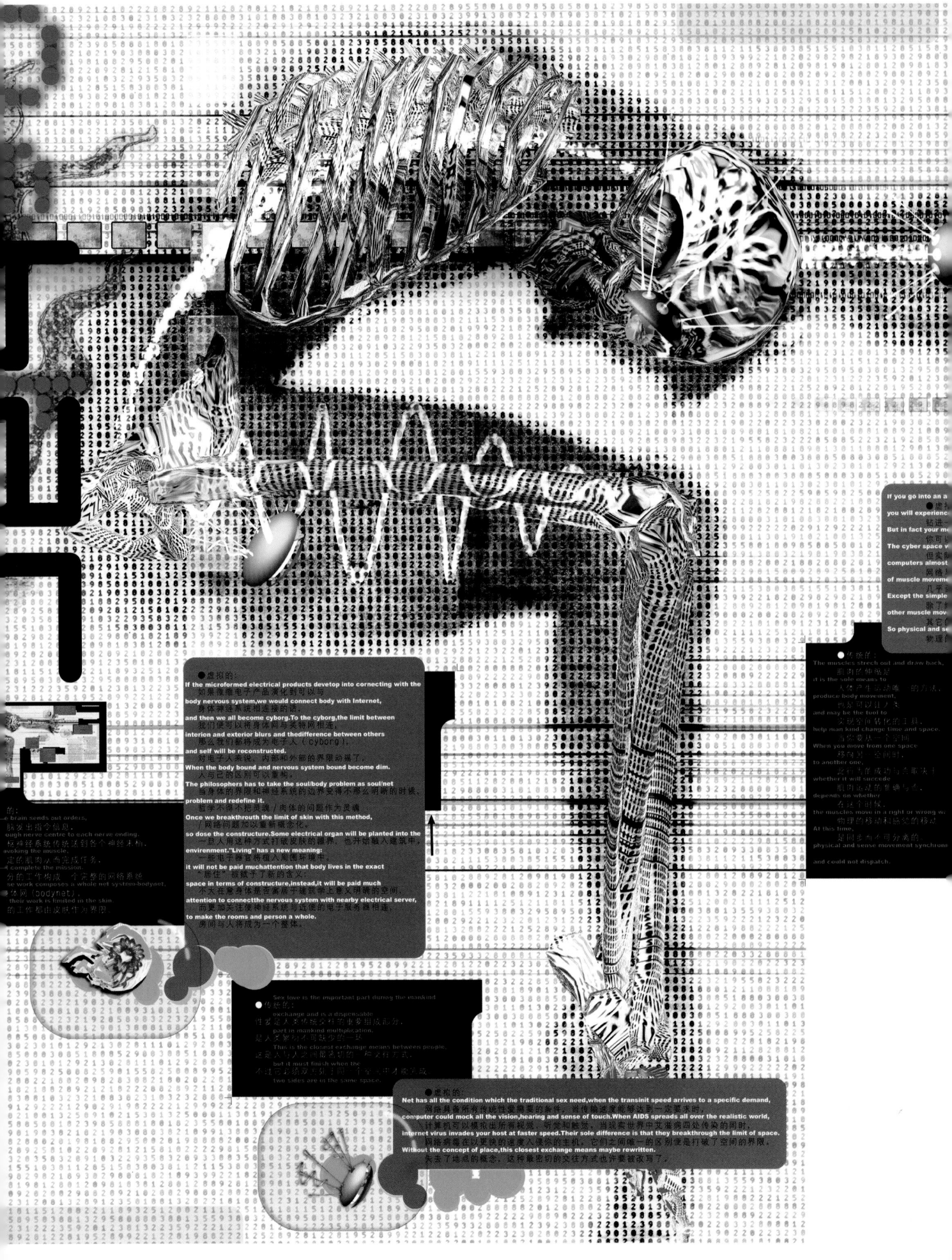
●虚拟的:
If the microformed electrical products devetop into cornecting with the
如果微型电子产品发展到可以
body nervous system,we would connect body with Internet,
将人体神经系统与因特网相连,
and then we all become cyborg.To the cyborg,the limit between
那么我们都将成为电子人(cyborg)。
interion and exterior blurs and thedifference between others
对电子人来说,内部和外部的界限模糊了,
and self will be reconstructed.
对电子人来说,内部和外部的界限模糊了,
When the body bound and nervous system bound become dim.
人与己的区别可以重构。
The philosophers has to take the soul/body problem as soul/net
当身体的外壳和神经系统的边界变得不够公明晰的时候,
problem and redefine it.
哲学家必须把灵魂/肉体的问题作为灵魂
Once we breakthroth the limit of skin with this method,
一旦人用这种方式打破皮肤的限界,
so dose the constructure.Some electrical organ will be planted into the
也开始重构人造躯干。
environement."Living" has a new meaning:
一些电子器官将植入周围环境中。
it will not be paid muchattention that body lives in the exact
"居住"有了新的含义。
space in terms of constructure,instead,it will be paid much
不大在意身体是否囿于建筑学上意义明确的空间,
attention to connectthe nervous system with nearby electrical server,
而更加关注使神经系统与就近的电子服务器相连,
to make the rooms and person a whole.
房间与人将成为一个整体。
●传统的:
Sex love is the important part during the mankind
性爱是人类繁衍的不可或少的一部
exchange and is a disposable
分,并非多姐技巧,
part in mankind multiplication.
是人类繁衍不可缺少的一部
This is the closest exchange means between people,
这是人与人之间最紧密的一种交往方式,
but it must finish when the
不过它必须要在别人同一个空间中才能完成
two sides are in the same space.
●虚拟的:
Net has all the condition which the traditional sex need,when the transinit speed arrives to a specific demand,
网络具备所有传统性爱需要的条件,当传输速度能够达到一定要求时,
computer could mock all the vision,hearing and sense of touch.When AIDS spreads all over the realistic world,
计算机可以模拟出所有视觉、听觉和触觉。当现实世界中艾滋病四处传染的同时,
internet virus invades your host at faster speed.Their sole difference is that they breakthrough the limit of space.
网络病毒在以更快的速度入侵你的主机,它们之间唯一的区别便是打破了空间的界限。
Without the concept of place,this closest exchange means maybe rewritten.
失去了地点的概念,这种最紧密的交往方式也许要被改写了。
If you go into an a
●传统
you will experienc
的交往
But in fact your me
你可以
The cyber space v
但实际
computers almost
网络与
of muscle moveme
几乎
Except the simple
除了
other muscle mov
其它
So physical and se
整理
●肌肉伸展:
The muscles stretch out and draw back,
肌肉伸缩是
it is the sole means to
人体产生运动唯一的方法,
produce body movement,
也是可以让人类
and may be the tool to
实现空间转化的工具,
help man kind change time and space.
当你要从一个空间
When you move from one space
移向另一空间时,
to another one,
是否成功与否取决于
whether it will succede
肌肉运动的准确与否,
depends on whether
在这个时候,
the muscles move in a right or wrong w
物理的移动和感觉的移动
At this time,
是同步而不可分离的,
physical and sense movement synchrone
and could not dispatch.

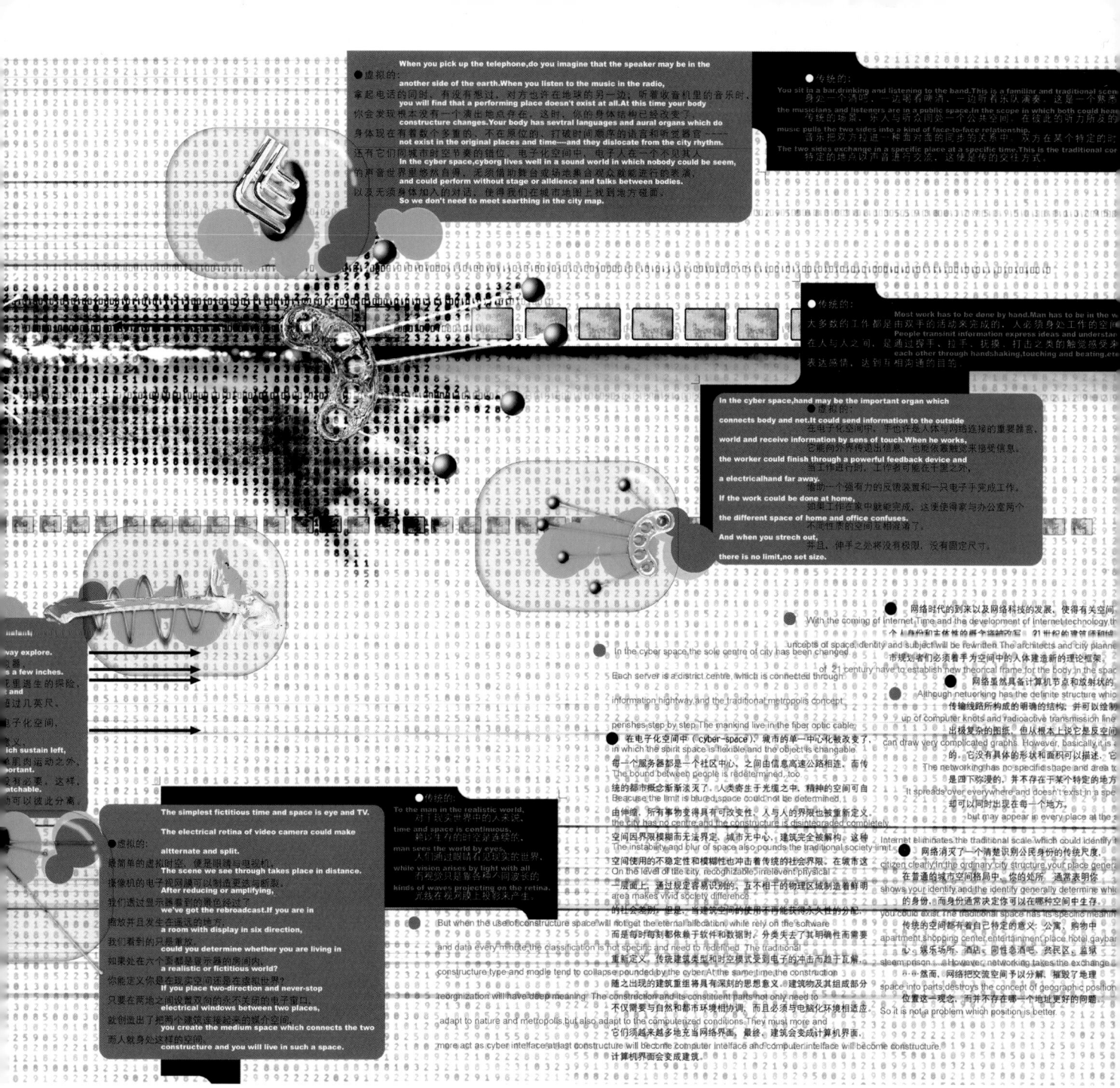
●虚拟的:
When you pick up the telephone,do you imagine that the speaker may be in the
another side of the earth.When you listen to the music in the radio,
you will find that a performing place doesn't exist at all.At this time your body
constructure changes.Your body has sevtral languages and aural organs which do
not exist in the original places and time---and they dislocate from the city rhythm.
In the cyber space,cyborg lives well in a sound world in which nobody could be seem,
and could perform without stage or alidience and talks between bodies.
So we don't need to meet searthing in the city map.
●传统的:
You sit in a bar,drinking and listening to the band.This is a familiar and traditional scen
the musicians and listeners are in a public space.In the scope in which both could hear
music pulls the two sides into a kind of face-to-face relationship.
The two sides exchange in a specific place at a specific time.This is the traditional cor
●传统的:
Most work has to be done by hand.Man has to be in the w
People transmit information express ideas and understan
each other through handshaking,touching and beating,etc
●虚拟的:
In the cyber space,hand may be the important organ which
connects body and net.It could send information to the outside
world and receive information by sens of touch.When he works,
the worker could finish through a powerful feedback device and
a electricalhand far away.
If the work could be done at home,
the different space of home and office confuses.
And when you strech out,
there is no limit,no set size.
●网络时代的到来以及网络科技的发展，使得有关空间
With the coming of Internet,Time and the development of Internet technology,th
uncepts of space identity and subject will be rewritten.The architects and city planne
of 21 century have to establish new theorical frame for the body in the spac
In the cyber space,the sole centre of city has been changed
Each server is a district centre, which is connected through
information hightway,and the traditional metropolis concept
perishes step by step.The mankind live in the fiber optic cable;
●在电子化空间中（cyber-space），城市的单一中心化被改变了，
in which the spirit space is flexible and the object is changable.
每一个服务器都是一个社区中心，之间由信息高速公路相连。而传
The bound between people is redetermined, too
统的都市概念渐渐淡灭了。人类寄生于光缆之中，精神的空间可自
Because the limit is blured,space could not be determined.
由伸缩，所有事物变得具有可改变性。人与人的界限也被重新定义。
the city has no centre,and the constructure is disintegrated completely
空间因界限模糊而无法界定，城市无中心，建筑完全被解构。这种
The instability and blur of space also pounds the traditional society imit
空间使用的不稳定性和模糊性也冲击着传统的社会界限。在城市这
On the level of the city, recognizable, irrelevent physical
一层面上，通过规定容易识别的，互不相干的物理区域制造着鲜明
area makes vivid society difference.
的社会差别。但是，当建筑空间的使用不再能获得永久性的分配，
But when the use of constructure space will not get the eternal allocation, while rely on the software
而是每时每刻都依赖于软件和数据时，分类失去了其明确性而需要
and data every minute,the classification is not specific and need to redefined.The traditional
重新定义。传统建筑类型和时空模式受到电子的冲击而趋于瓦解，
constructure type and mode tend to collapse pounded by the cyber.At the same time,the construction
随之出现的建筑重组将具有深刻的思想意义。建筑物及其组成部分
reorgnization will have deep meaning.The construction and its constituent parts not only need to
不仅需要与自然和都市环境相协调，而且必须与电脑化环境相适应。
adapt to nature and metropolis but also adapt to the computerized conditions.They must more and
它们须越来越多地充当网络界面，最终，建筑会变成计算机界面，
more act as cyber intelface at last constructure will become computer intelface and computer intelface will become constructure.
计算机界面会变成建筑。
●传统的:
To the man in the realistic world,
时空现实世界中的人来说，
time and space is continuous,
稳定生存的时空是连续的，
man sees the world by eyes,
人有通过眼睛看见现实的世界，
while vision arises by light with all
有视觉只是靠各种不同波长的
kinds of waves projecting on the retina.
光线在视网膜上投影才产生。
The simplest fictitious time and space is eye and TV.
The electrical retina of video camera could make
●虚拟的:
altternate and split.
最简单的虚拟时空，便是眼睛与电视机。
The scene we see through takes place in distance.
After reducing or amplifying,
we've got the rebroadcast.If you are in
a room with display in six direction,
could you determine whether you are living in
a realistic or fictitious world?
If you place two-direction and never-stop
electrical windows between two places,
you create the medium space which connects the two
constructure and you will live in such a space.
Internet eliminates the traditional scale which could identify
citizen clearly.In the ordinary city structure,your place gener
shows your identity,and the identify generally determine whic
you could exist.The traditional space has its specific meanin
apartment,shopping center,entertainment place,hotel,gaybar
steam prison.However,networking takes the exchange
space into parts,destroys the concept of geographic position
So it is not a problem which position is better.
●网络消灭了一个清楚识别公民身份的传统尺度。
在普通的城市空间格局中，你的处所，通常表明你
的身份。而身份通常决定你可以在哪种空间中生存。
传统的空间都有着自己特定的意义：公寓，购物中
心，娱乐场所，酒店，同性恋酒吧，去民区，监狱
然而，网络把交流空间予以分解，摧毁了地理
位置这一观念，而并不存在哪一个地址更好的问题。

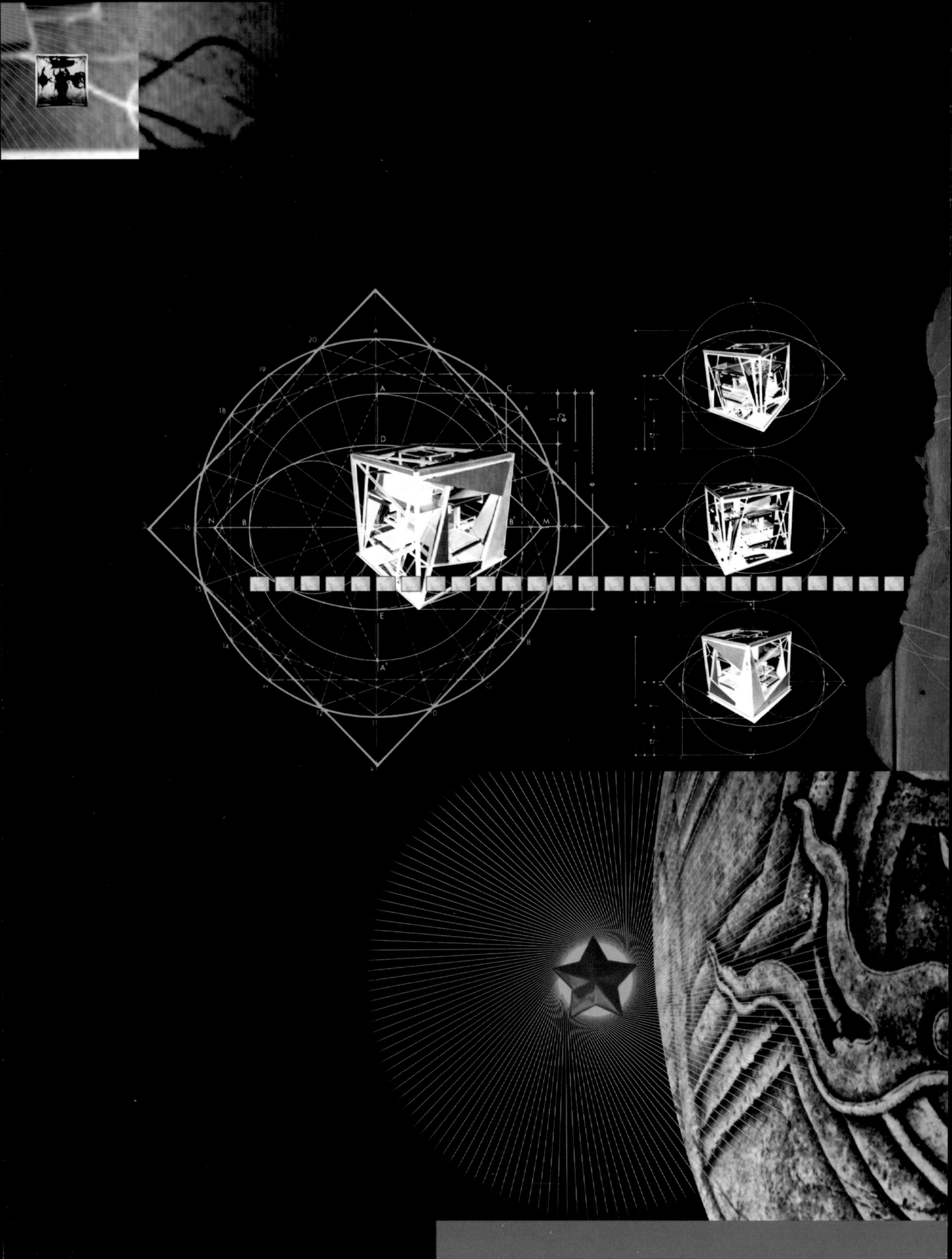

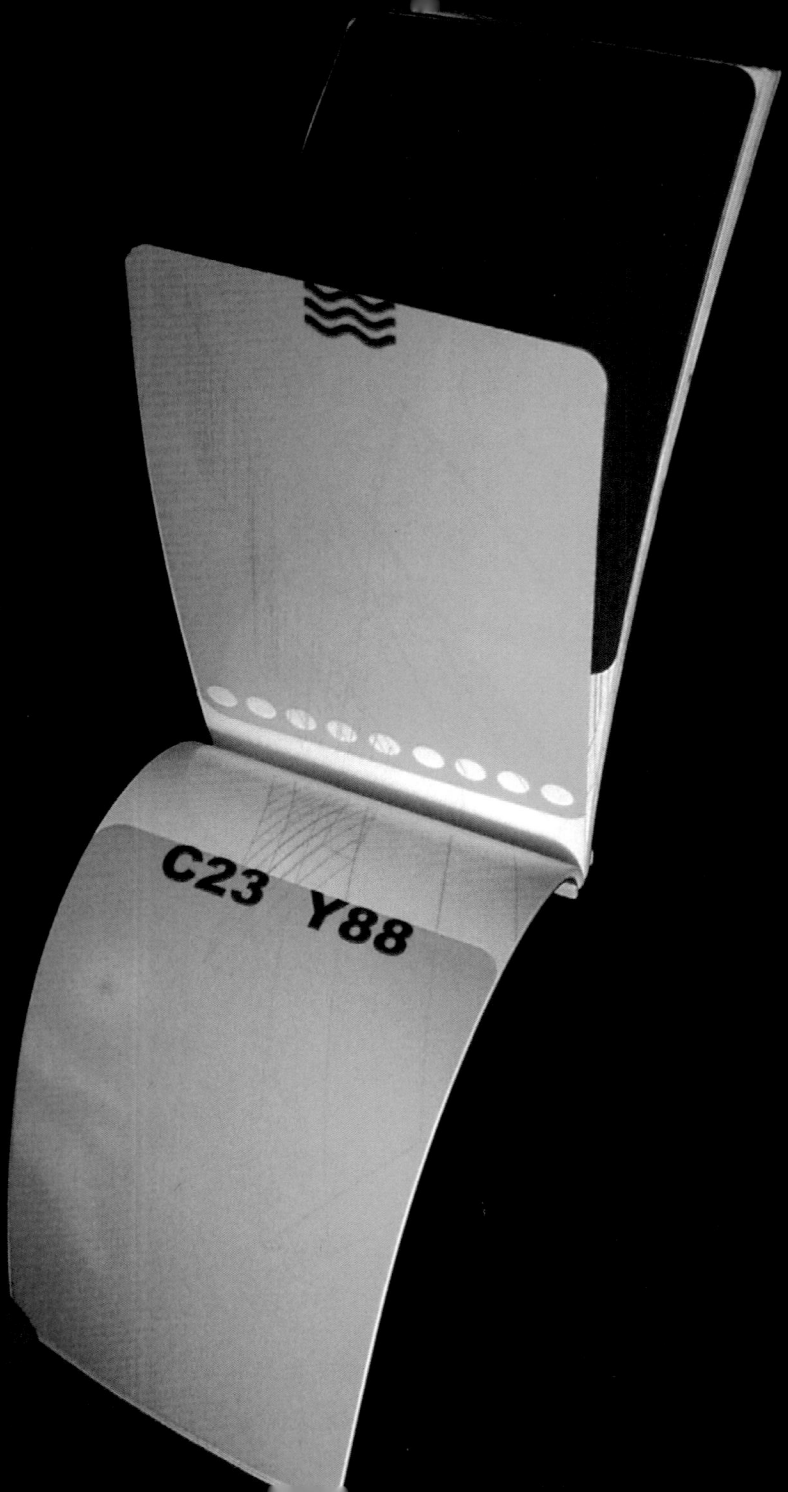
C23 Y88

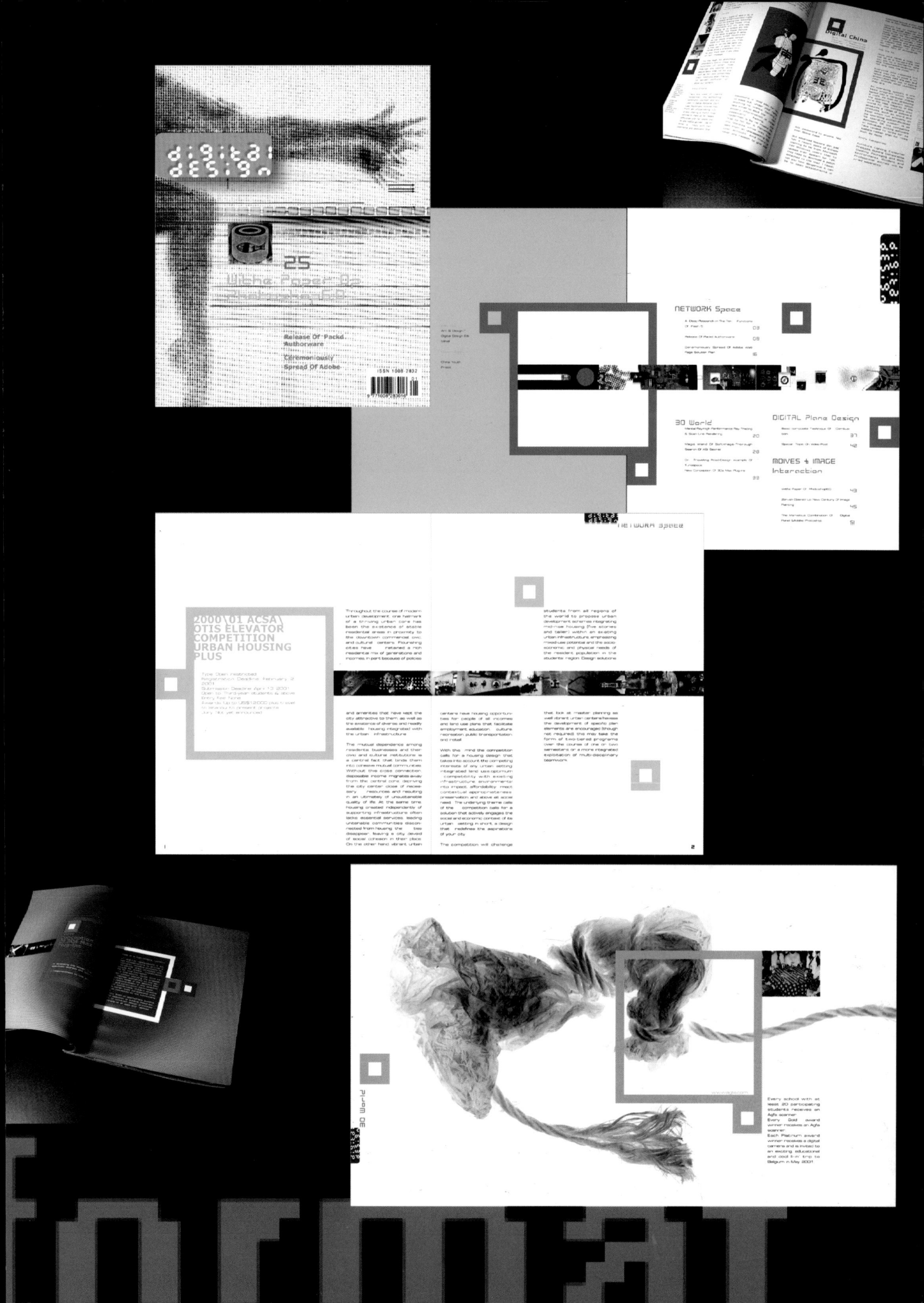
digital China
25
Release Of Packd. Authorware
Ceremoniously Spread Of Adobe
ISBN 1508 2832
NETWORK Space
3D World
DIGITAL Plane Design
MOVES + IMAGE Interaction
NETWORK SPACE
2000\01 ACSA\ OTIS ELEVATOR COMPETITION URBAN HOUSING PLUS
3D World

刘 宓

1977 年生于北京，曾就读于中央工艺美术学院附中
中央美术学院附中，中央美术学院设计系

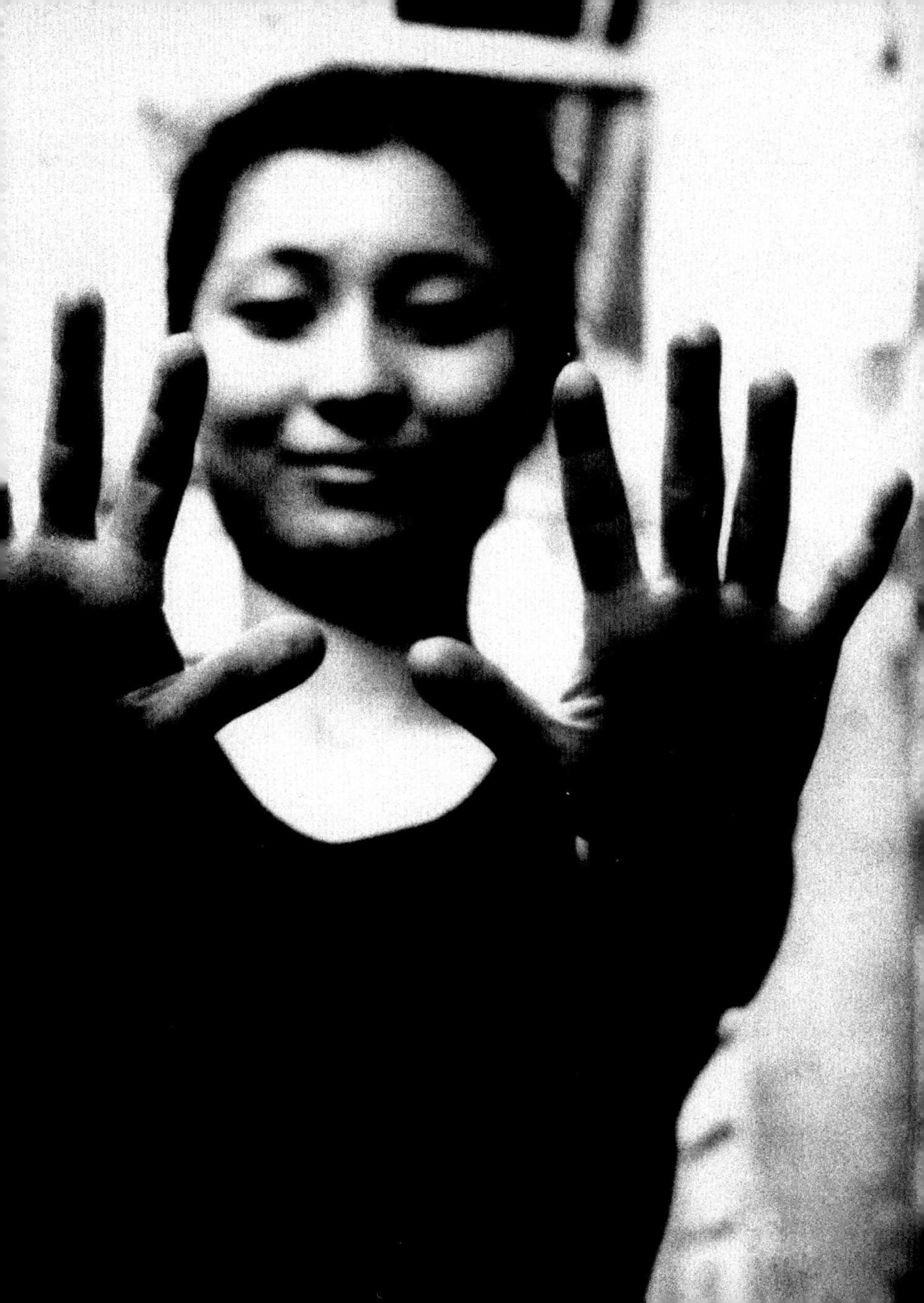

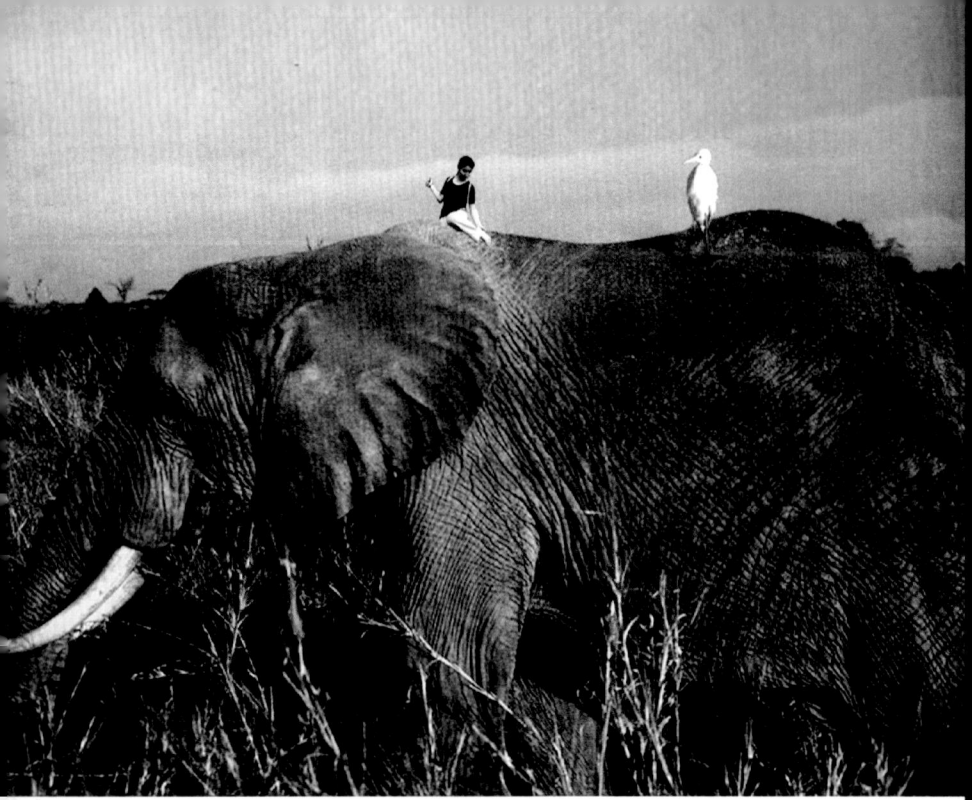

像很多大型动物一样
大象很欢迎专食昆虫的小鸟
没有鸟的帮助
它很难摆脱成群昆虫带来的困扰
越是庞大的结构
越需要细致入微的料理

*刘宏身高 1522毫米

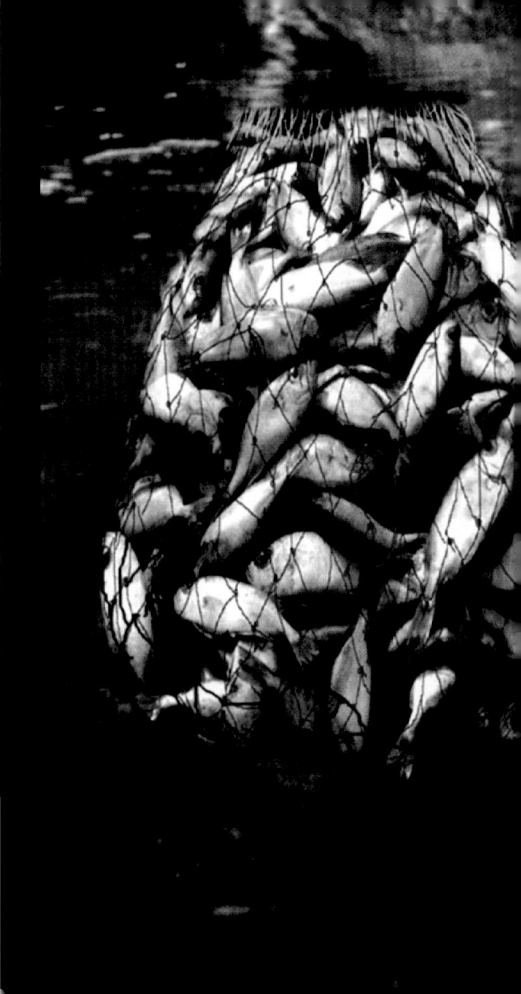

漏网之鱼

一网打尽了吗
一举一动虽不引人注目
关键时刻却能游刃有余

*刘彦身高 1522 毫米

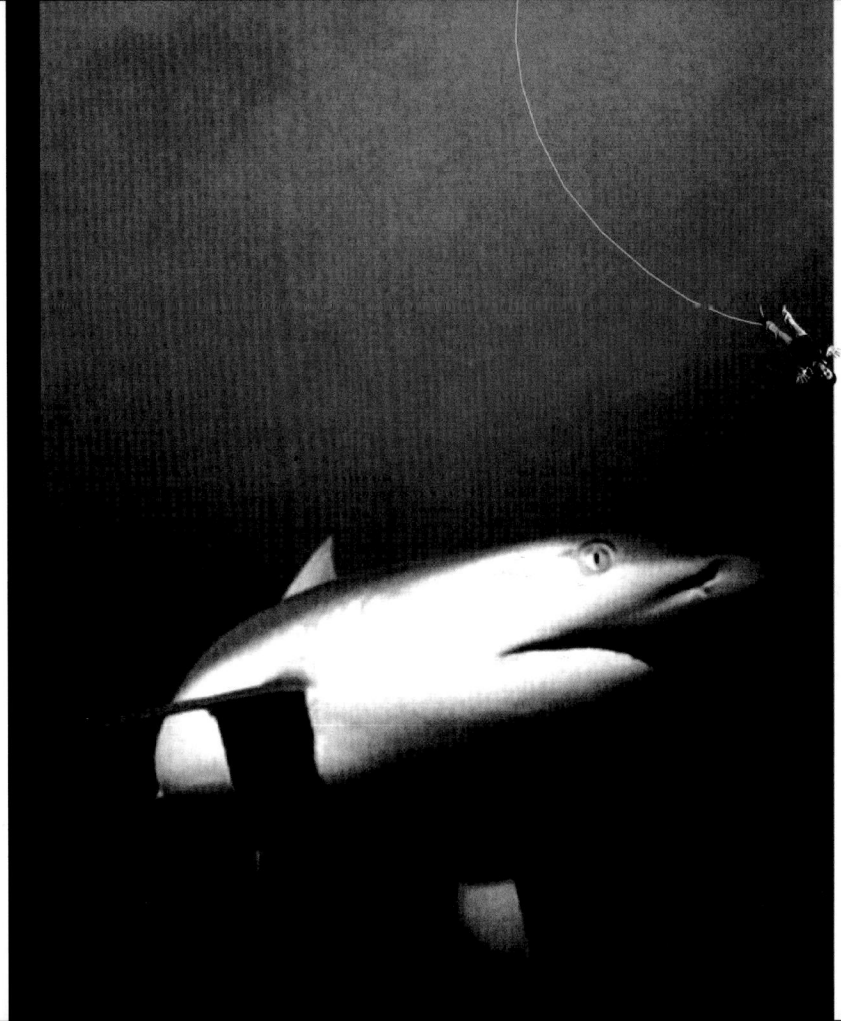

小也有诱惑力

想钓大鱼
你的诱饵并不需要太大
面对庞大的对象
小诱饵能投其所好
依靠特有的动态
色彩 气味及别的本领
它可以具有强大的吸引力
有诱惑力
就能以最小的代价钓到大鱼

*刘彦身高 1522 毫米

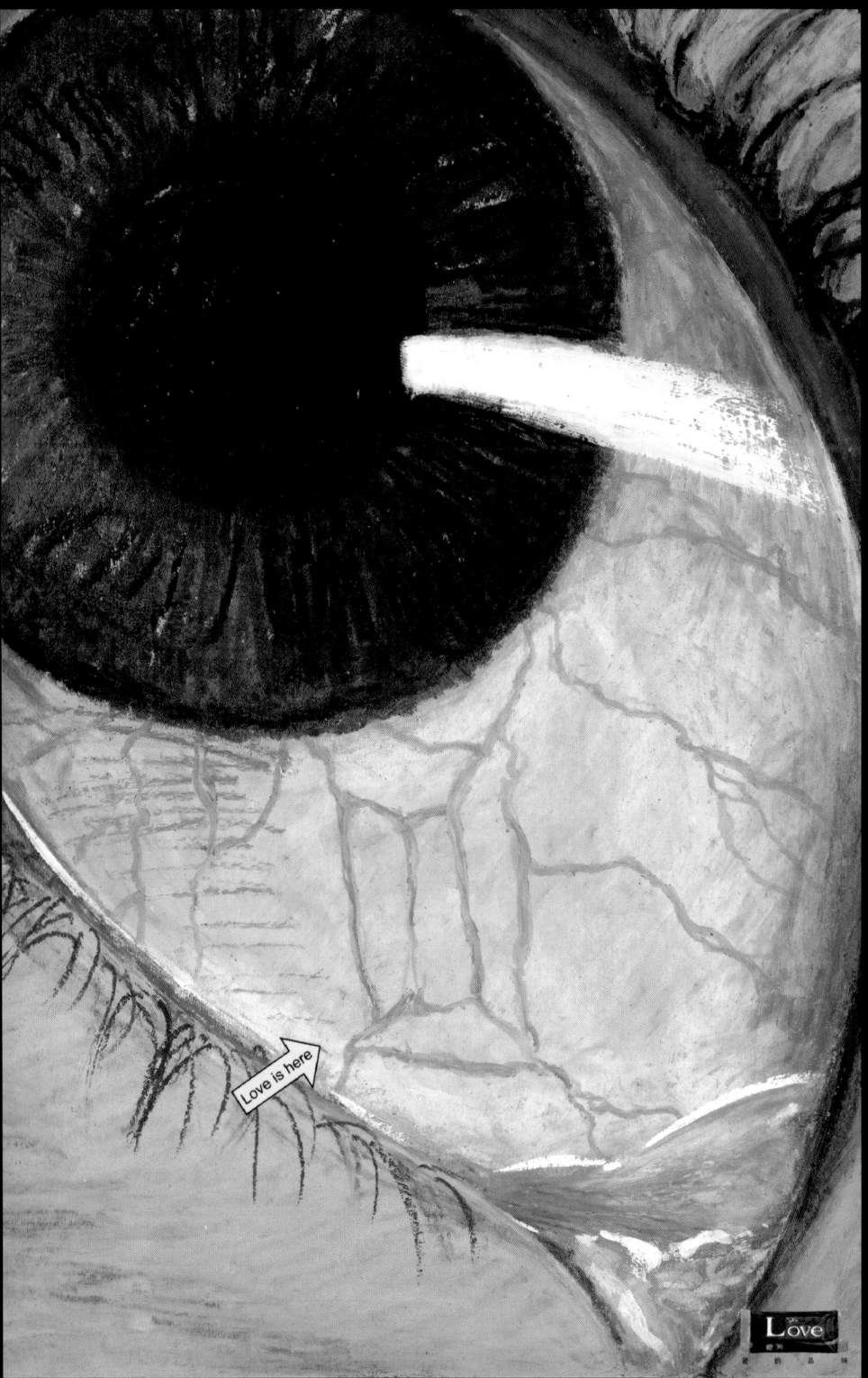
Love is here
Love

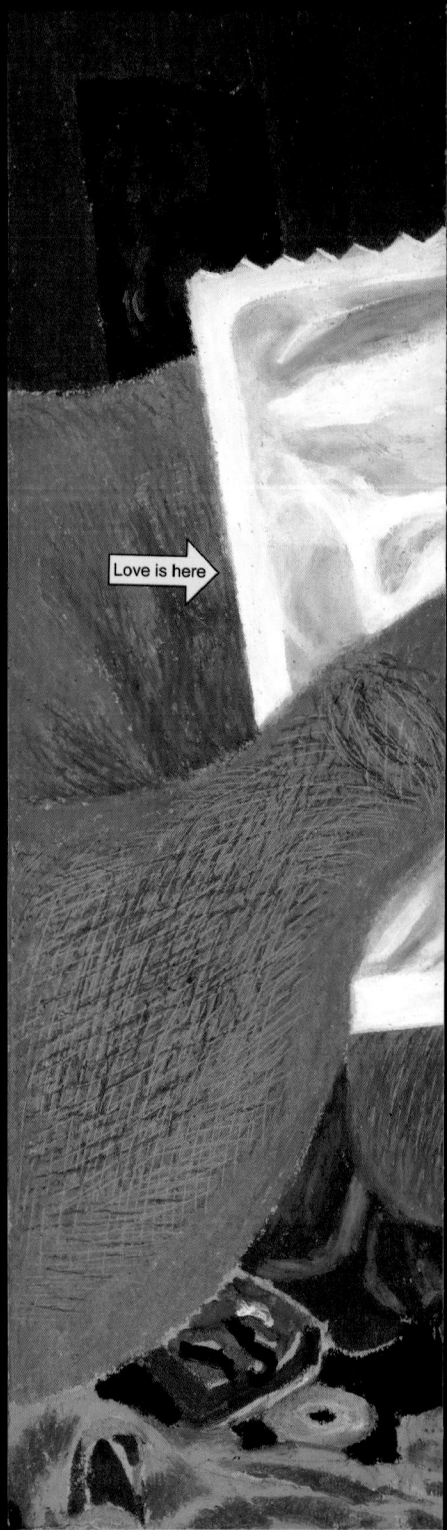
Love is here

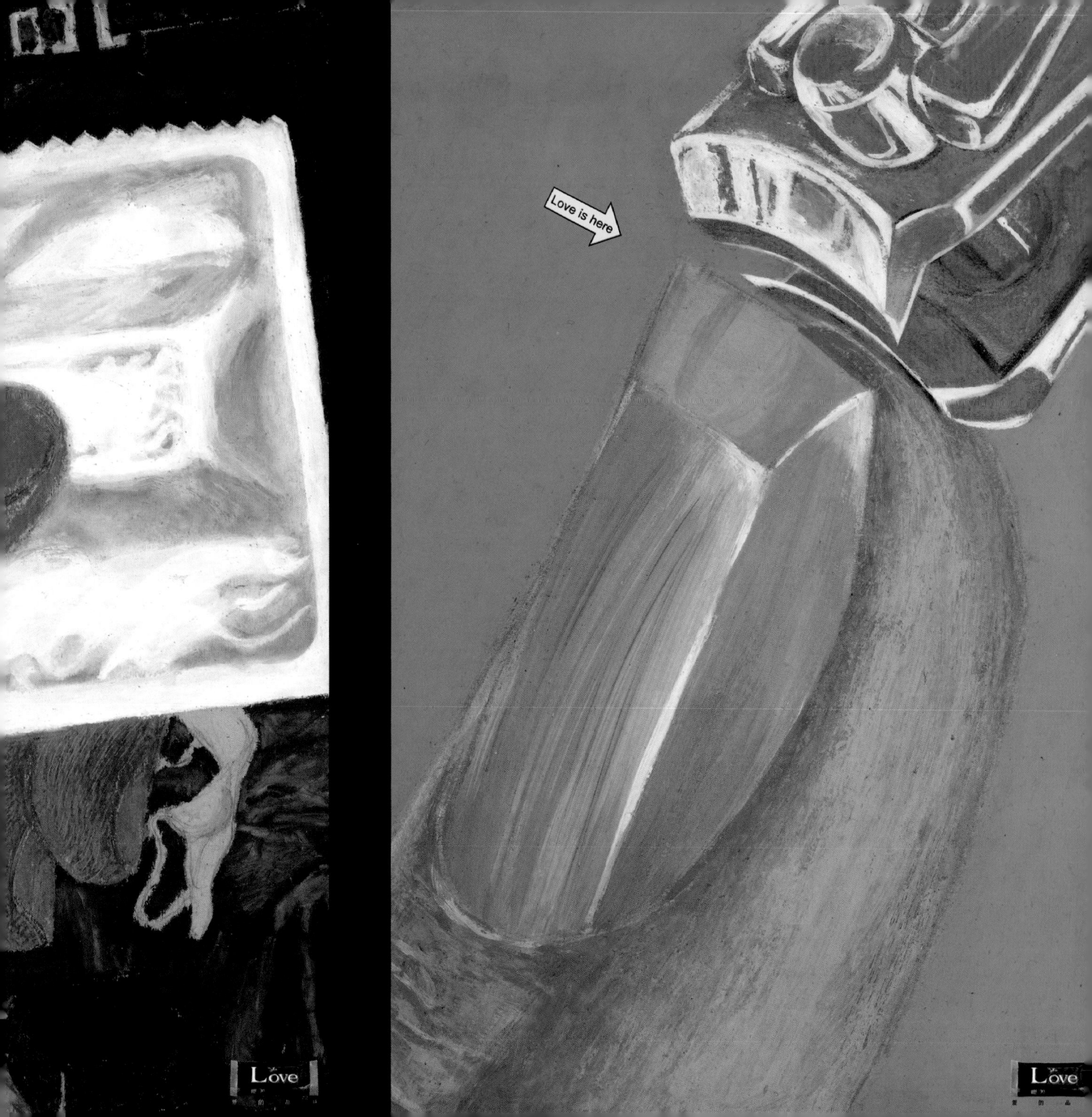
Love is here
Love
Love

胡晓媛

1977 年 12 月 8 日生于哈尔滨

1994 年 9 月考入中央美术学院附中

1996 年 作品《九件》获吴作人基金会优秀习作奖

1998 年 9 月考入中央美术学院设计系至今

1999 年 作品《禁锢》入选《新艺术后援——70 年代后》作品集

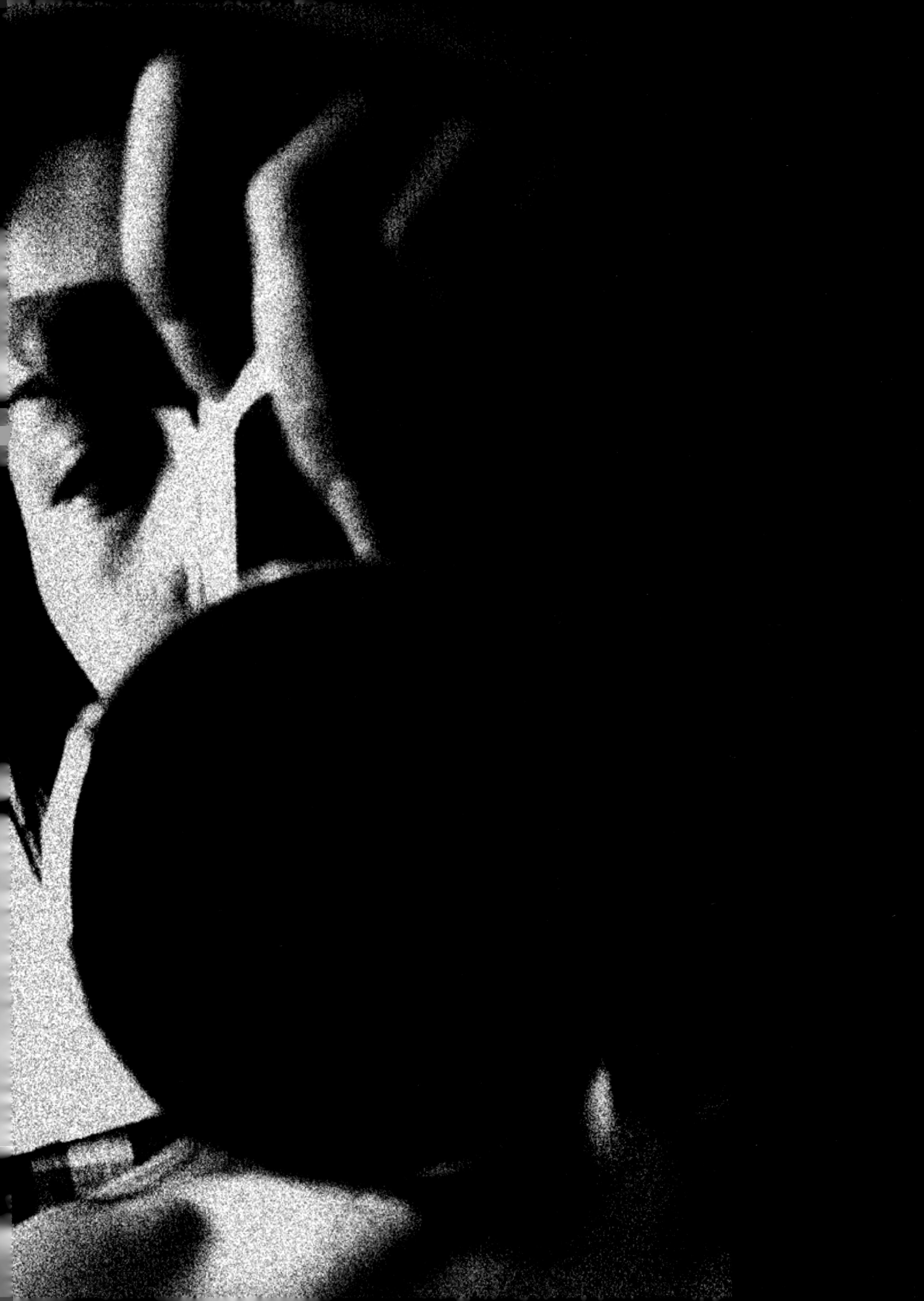

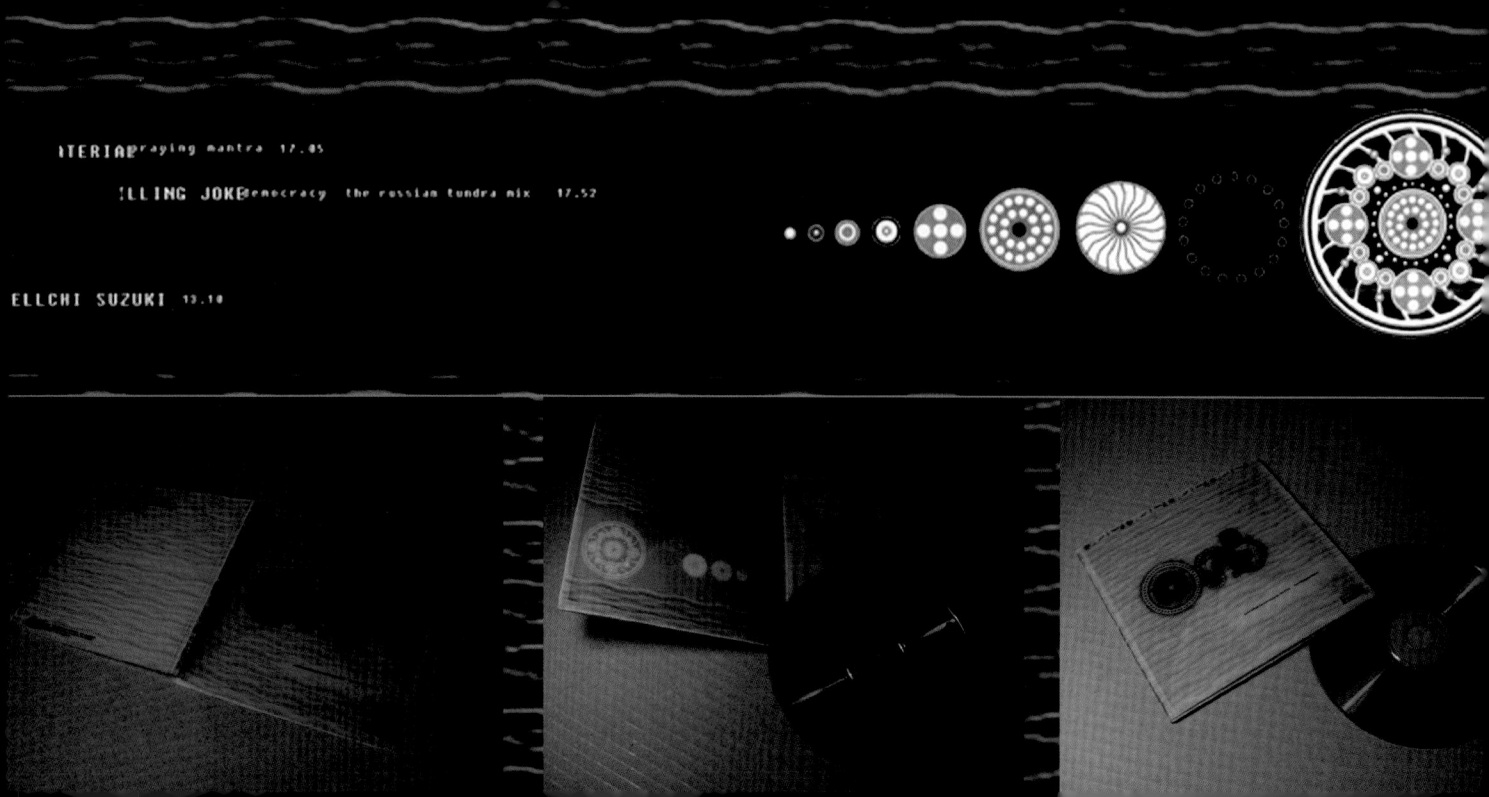
ITERIA praying mantra 17.05
!LLING JOKE democracy the russian tundra mix 17.52
ELLCHI SUZUKI 13.10

Auntie Aubrey's Excursions Beyond the Call of Duty

The Orb Remix Project

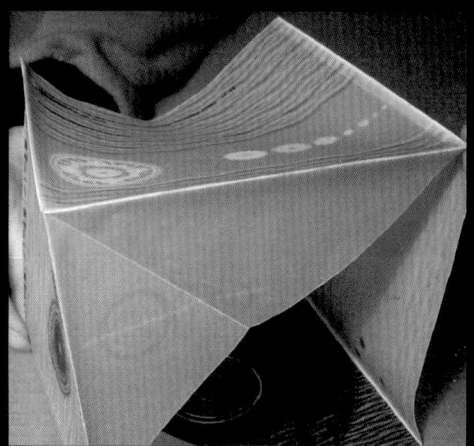

Serengeti 13.50 Trans Asian Express Mix (Ellchi Tatsuki)

weather vacuum 12.58 Orb Extended Remix (B Bloom/D Meller)

25 Logical Mix (Hrdger/Edwards)

7.08 Orbital Mix (Al Garwe)

rey's Excursions Beyond the Call of Duty

©1996 Deviant Records_BM
Records_22-23 Brook Mews
ated in the UK by Vital.

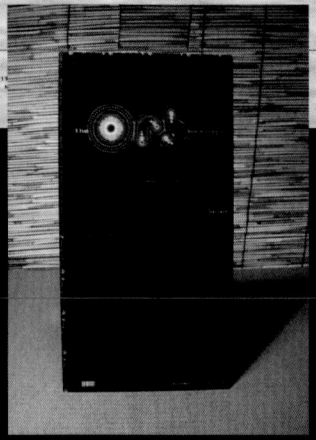

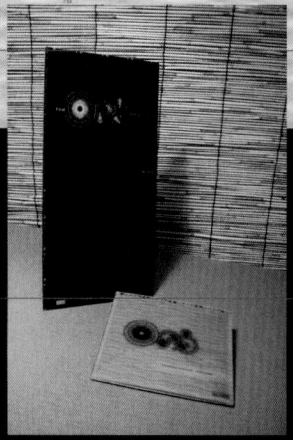

Auntie Aubrey's Excursions Beyond the Call of Duty The

ATERIAL Praying mantra 17.05

ELLING JOKE Democracy the russian tundra mix 17.52

ELLCHI SUZUKI 13.10

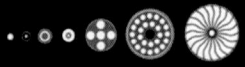

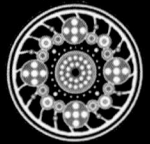

Auntie Aubrey's Excursions Beyond the Call of Duty The Orb Remix Project

The

Auntie Aubrey's Excursions Beyond the Call of Duty The Orb Remix Project

Auntie Aubrey's Excursions Beyond the Call of Duty

The

Aur

Excursions Beyond the Call of Duty The Orb Remix

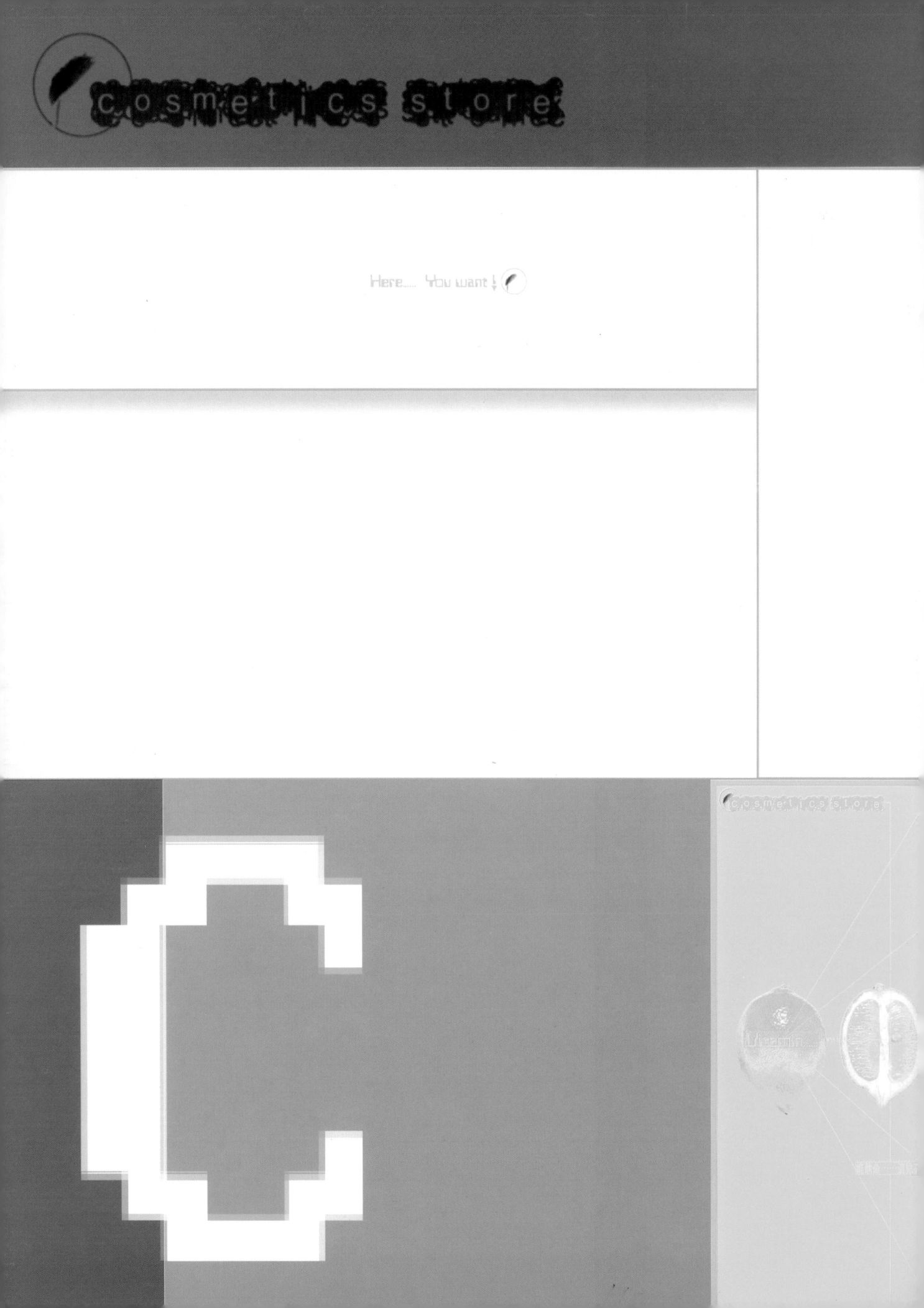
cosmetics store
Here..... You want !
cosmetics store

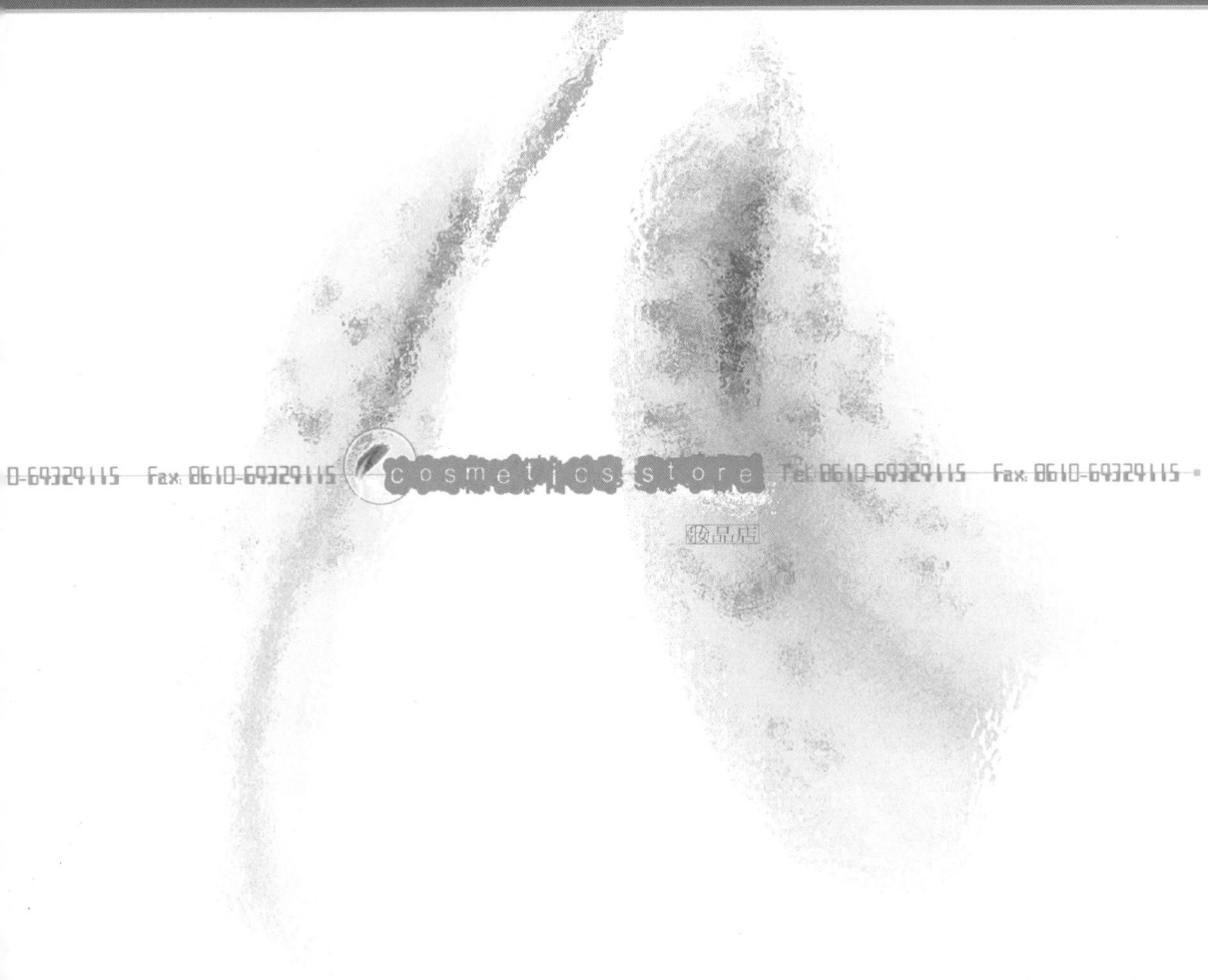
0-69329115 Fax: 0610-69329115
cosmetics store
Tel: 0610-69329115 Fax: 0610-69329115
极品店

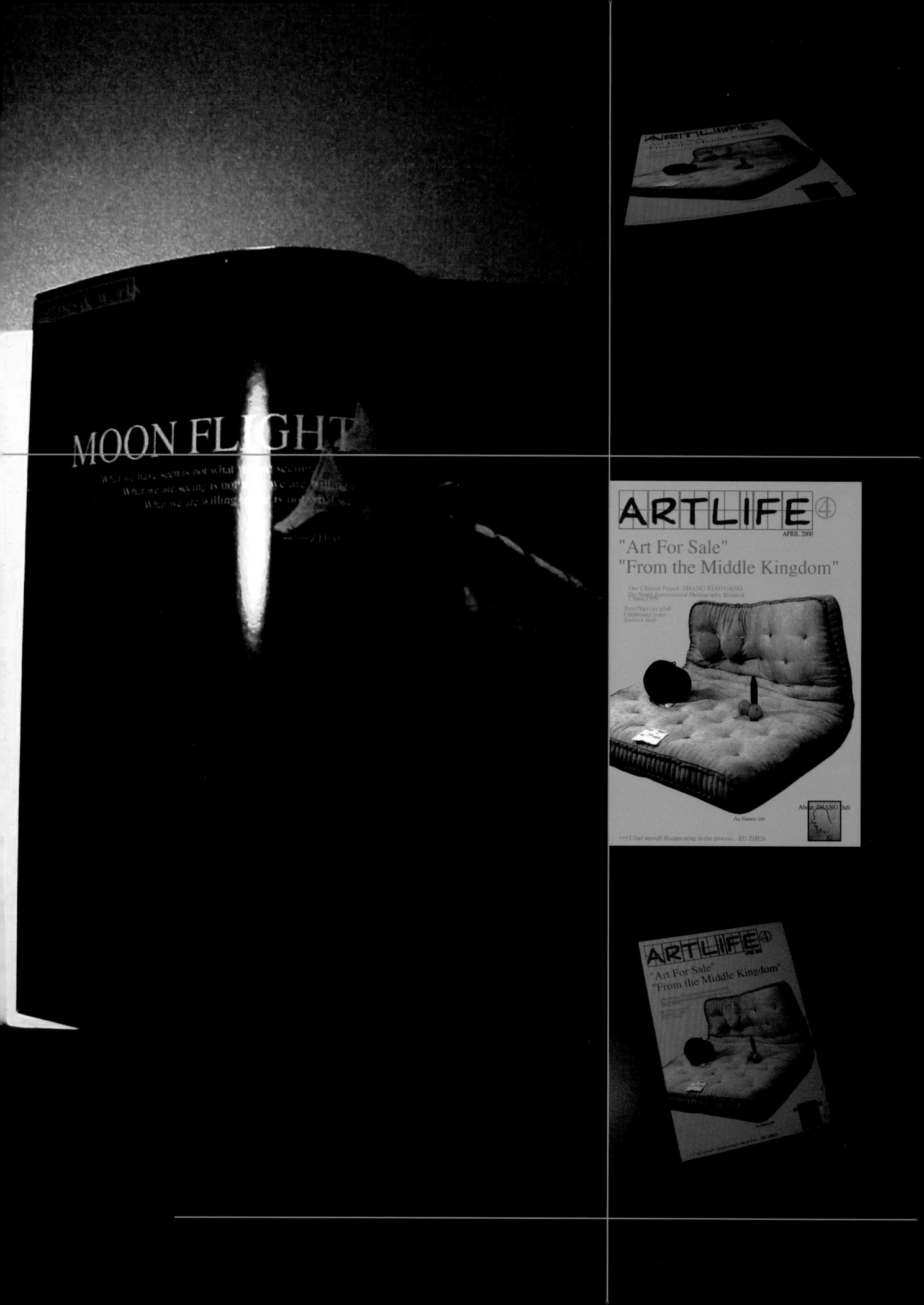
MOON FLIGHT
ARTLIFE ④
APRIL 2000
"Art For Sale"
"From the Middle Kingdom"
Our Chinese Friend -ZHANG XIAO GANG
The Ninth International Photography Biennial
Chang'ing
Zuvr7hyvsyt gfu8
Ghhbnuo tyuer
Jeerver dotk
Au Naewe 100
About ZHANG Dali
>>> I find myself disappearing in the process. -XU ZHEN
ARTLIFE ④
"Art For Sale"
"From the Middle Kingdom"

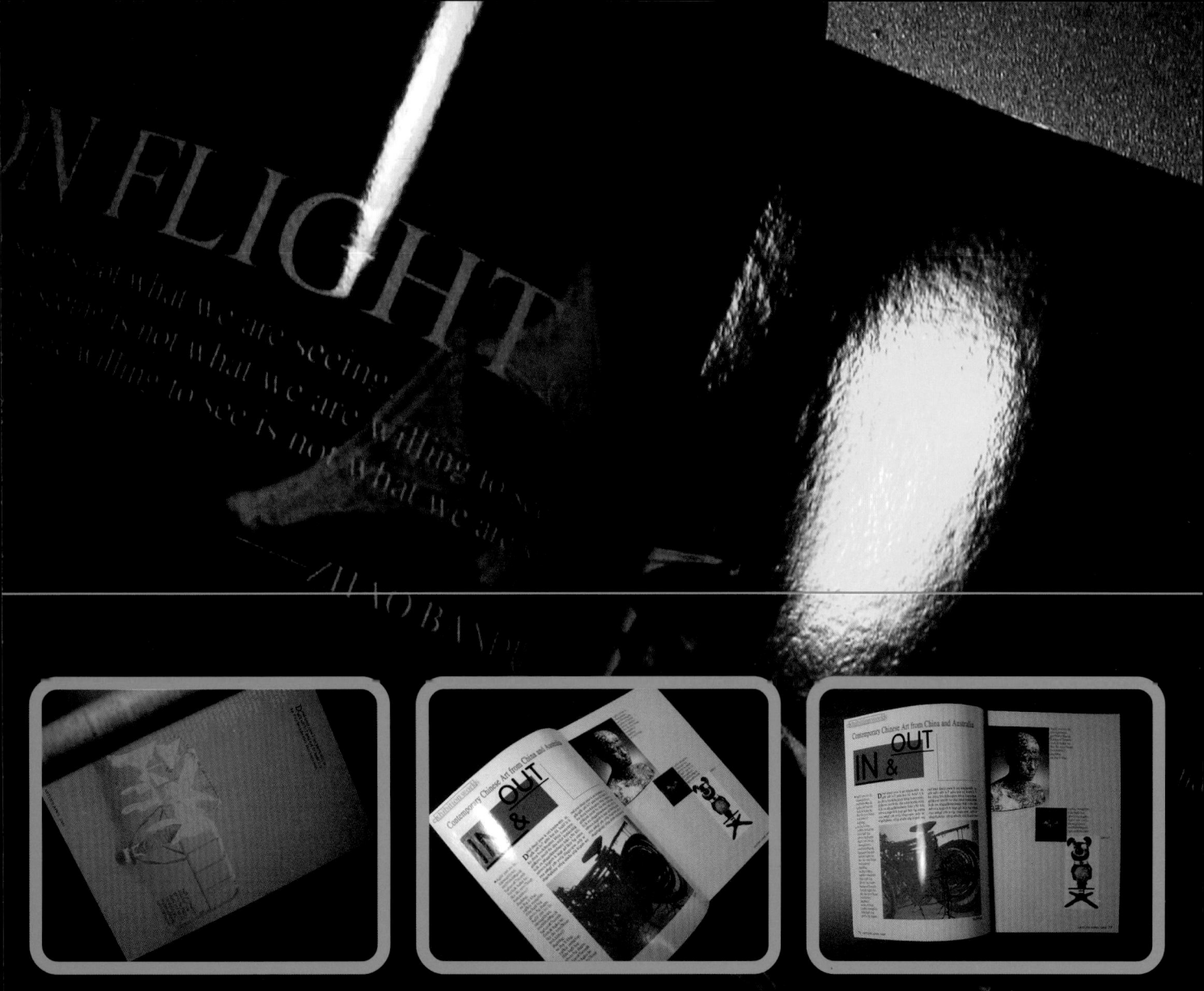
FLIGHT
Contemporary Chinese Art from China and Australia
IN & OUT

王 艳

1979 年出生于辽宁省大连市

1997 年考入中央美术学院平面设计专业

观念书籍设计《福尔摩斯探案集》曾获“第五届书籍装帧艺术展探索奖”，作品曾在北京中国美术馆、桂林及昆明等地展出

作品《展望 2000》获“惠普杯大赛”入围奖

《饕餮美餐》曾获金牍奖北京地区入围奖

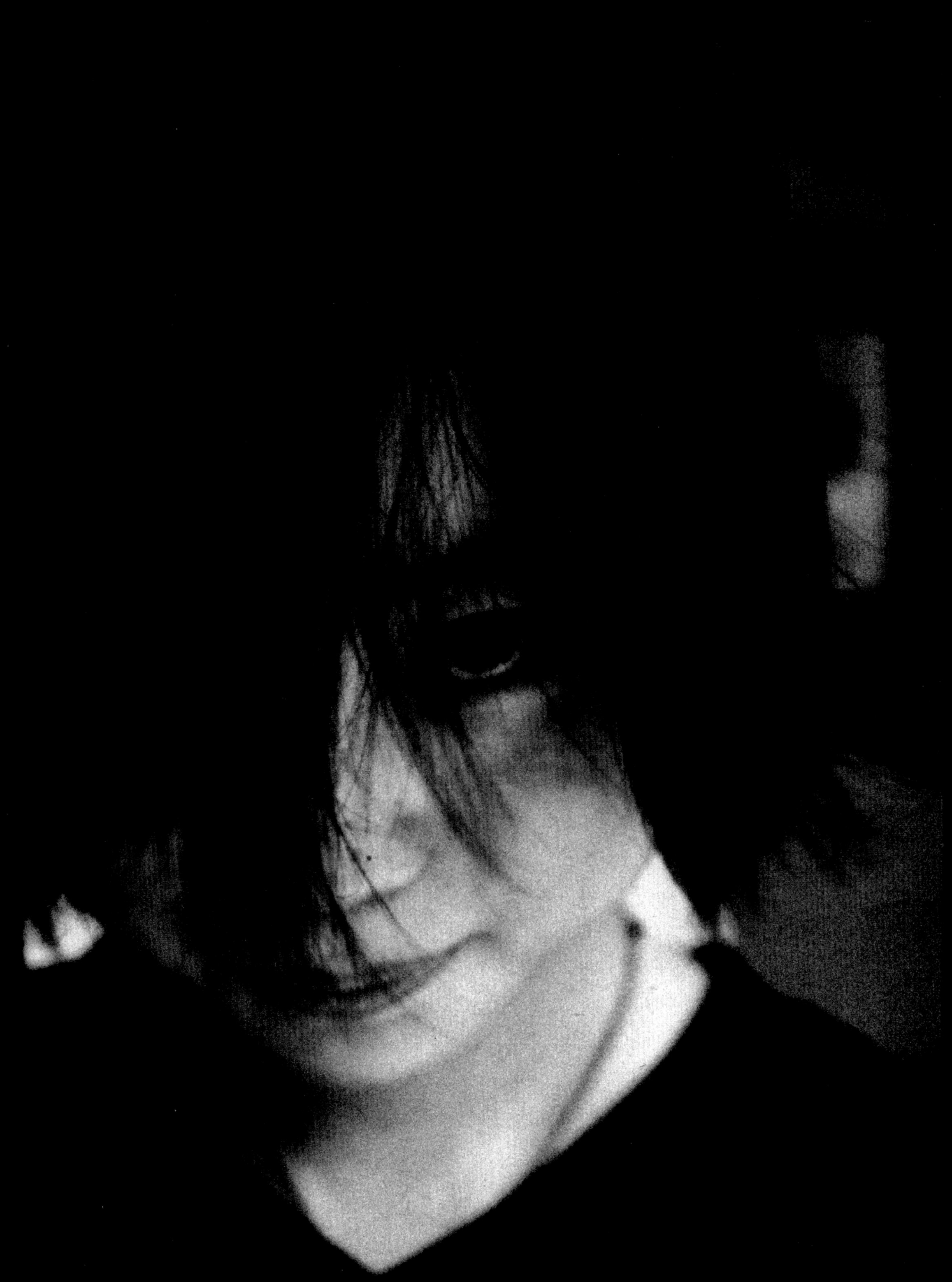

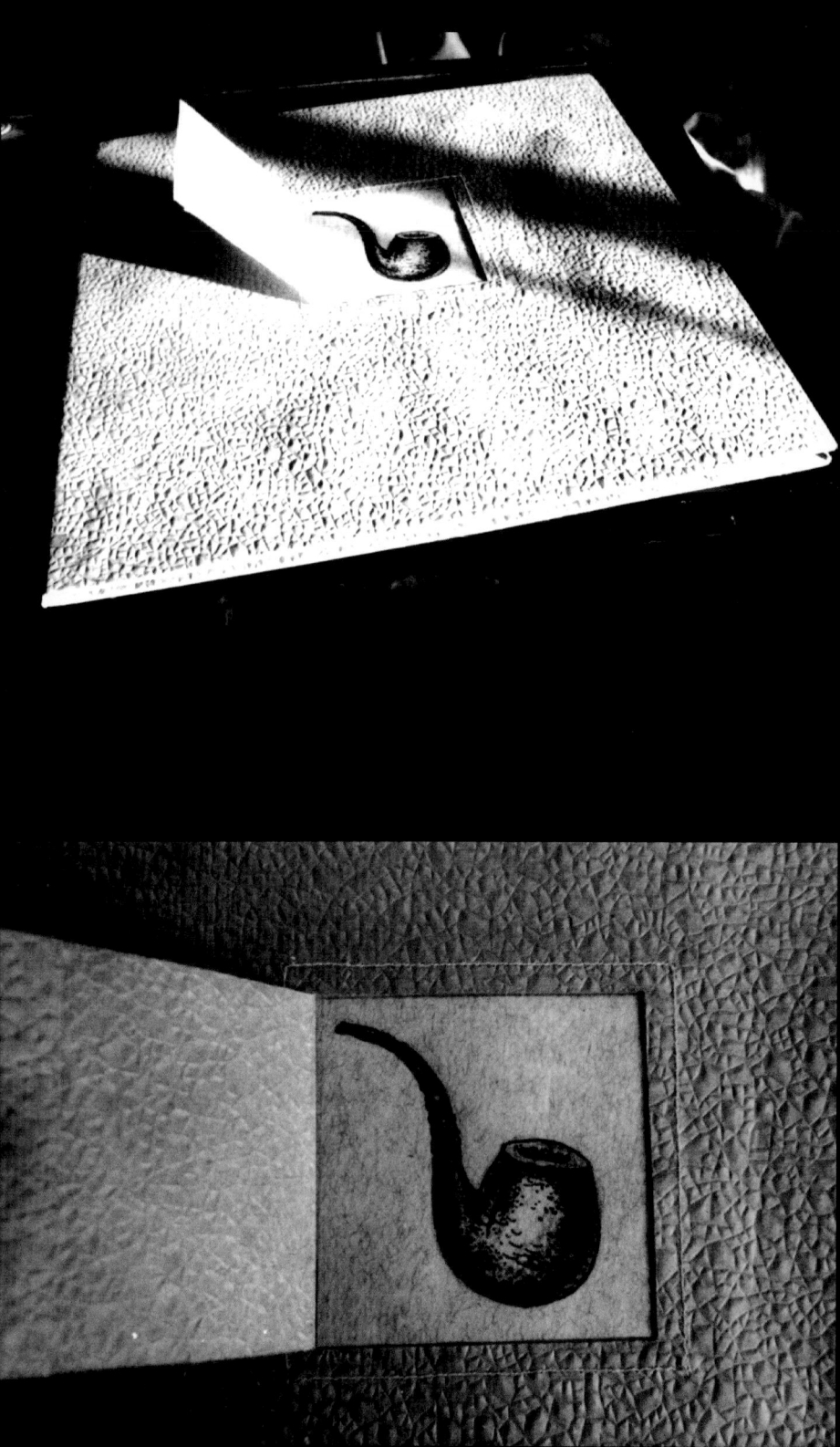

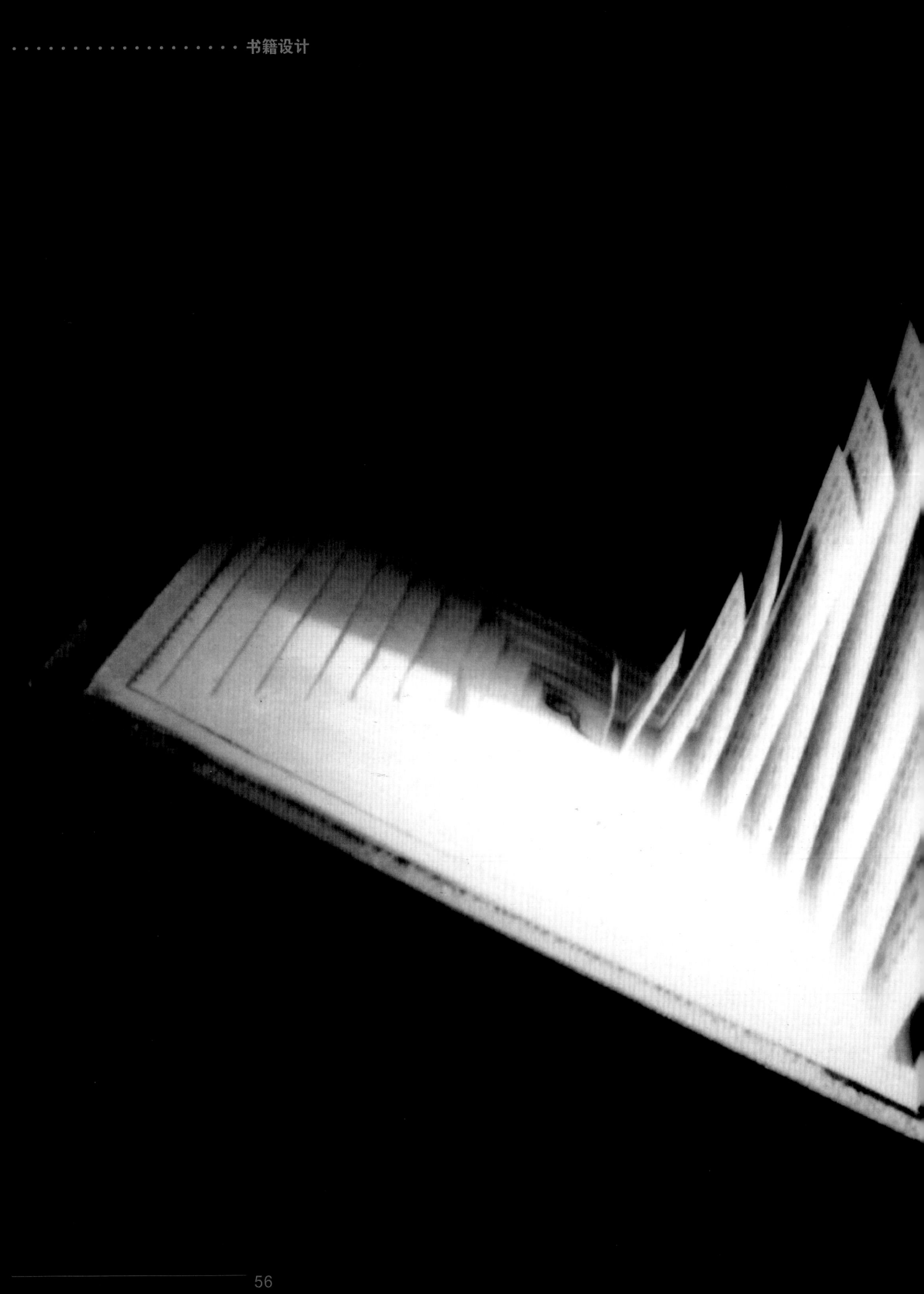

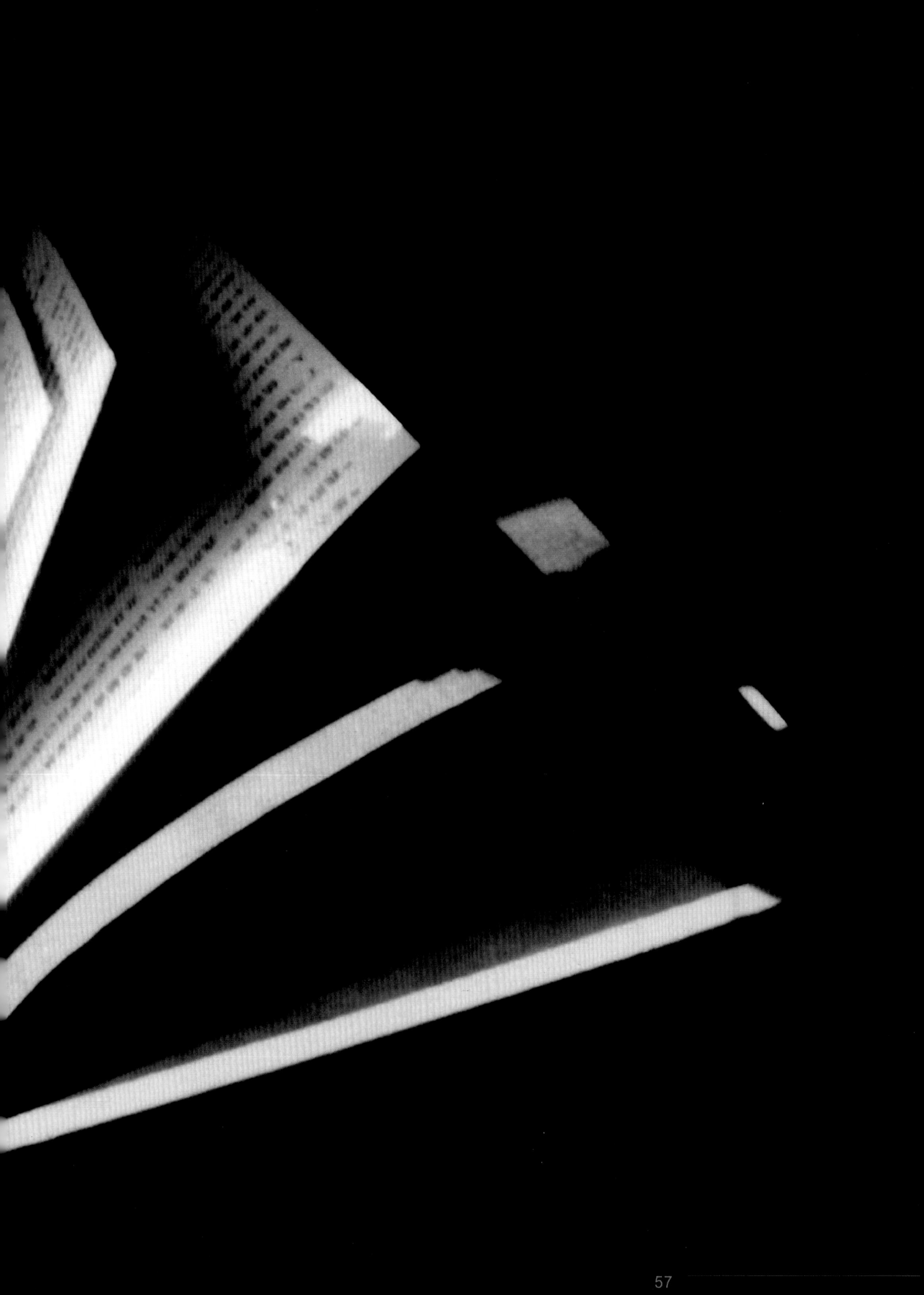

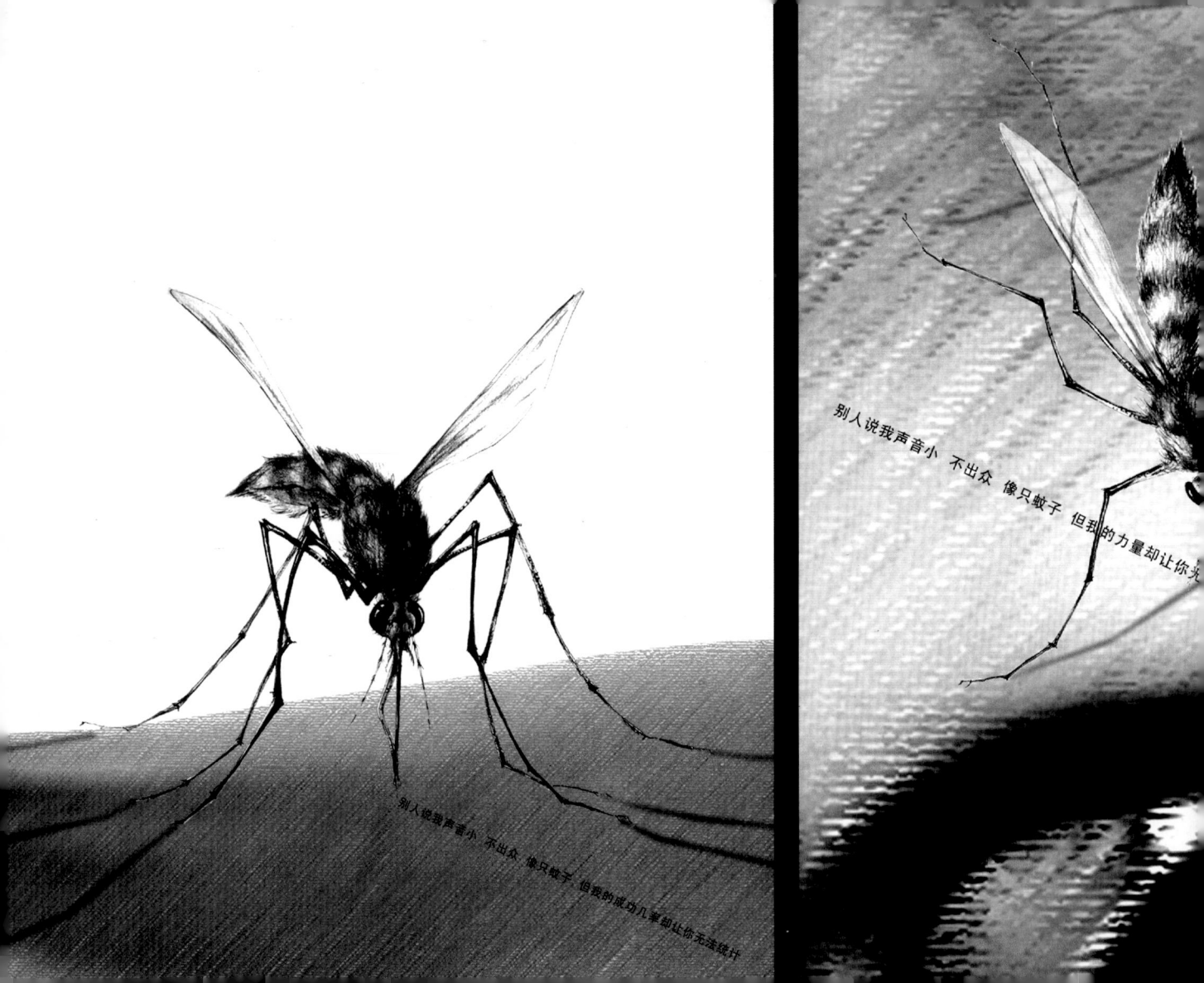
别人说我声音小 不出众 像只蚊子 但我的成功几率却让你无法统计
别人说我声音小 不出众 像只蚊子 但我的力量却让你无

别人说我声音小 不出众 像只蚊子 但我的本领让他无法忽视

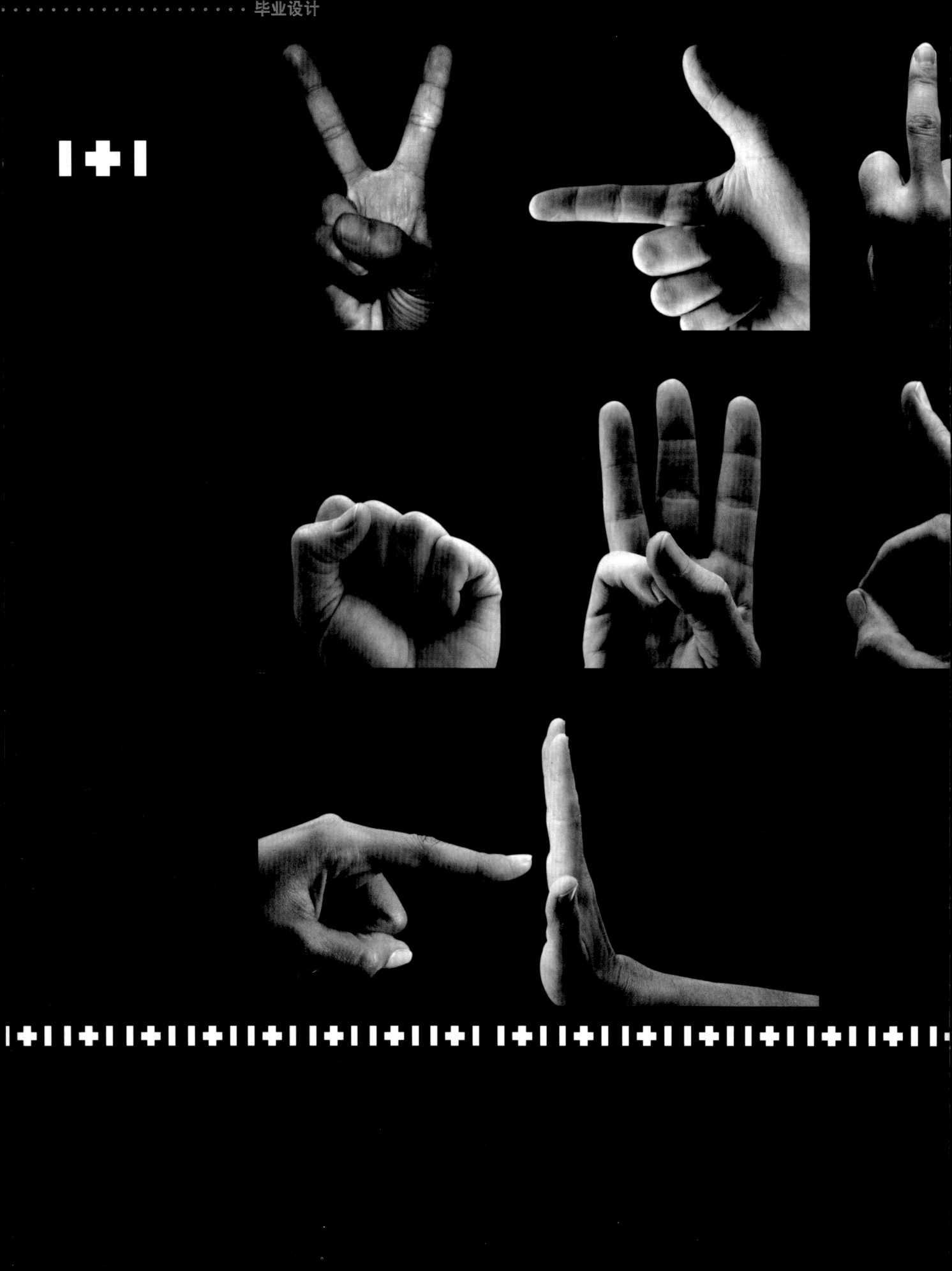

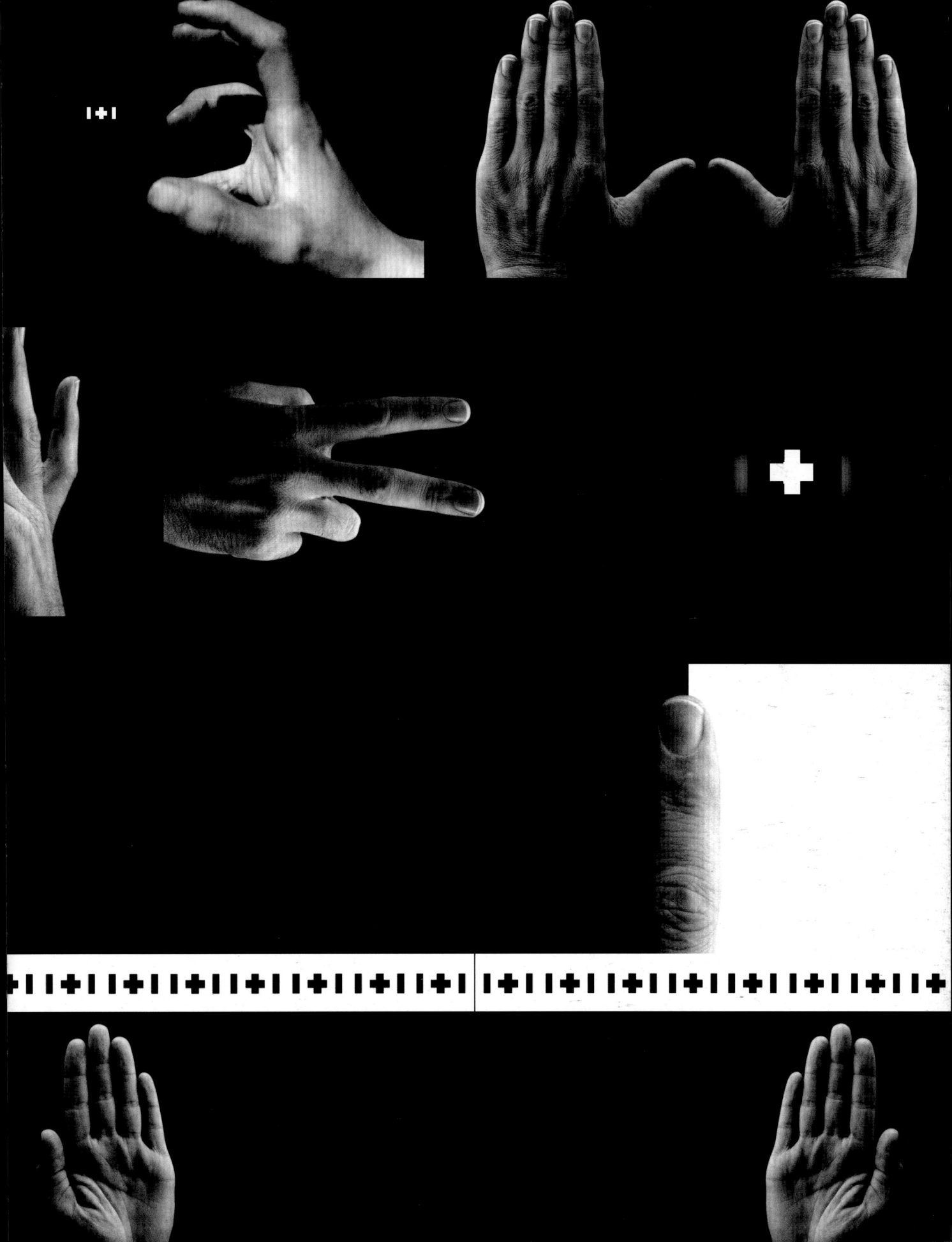

G

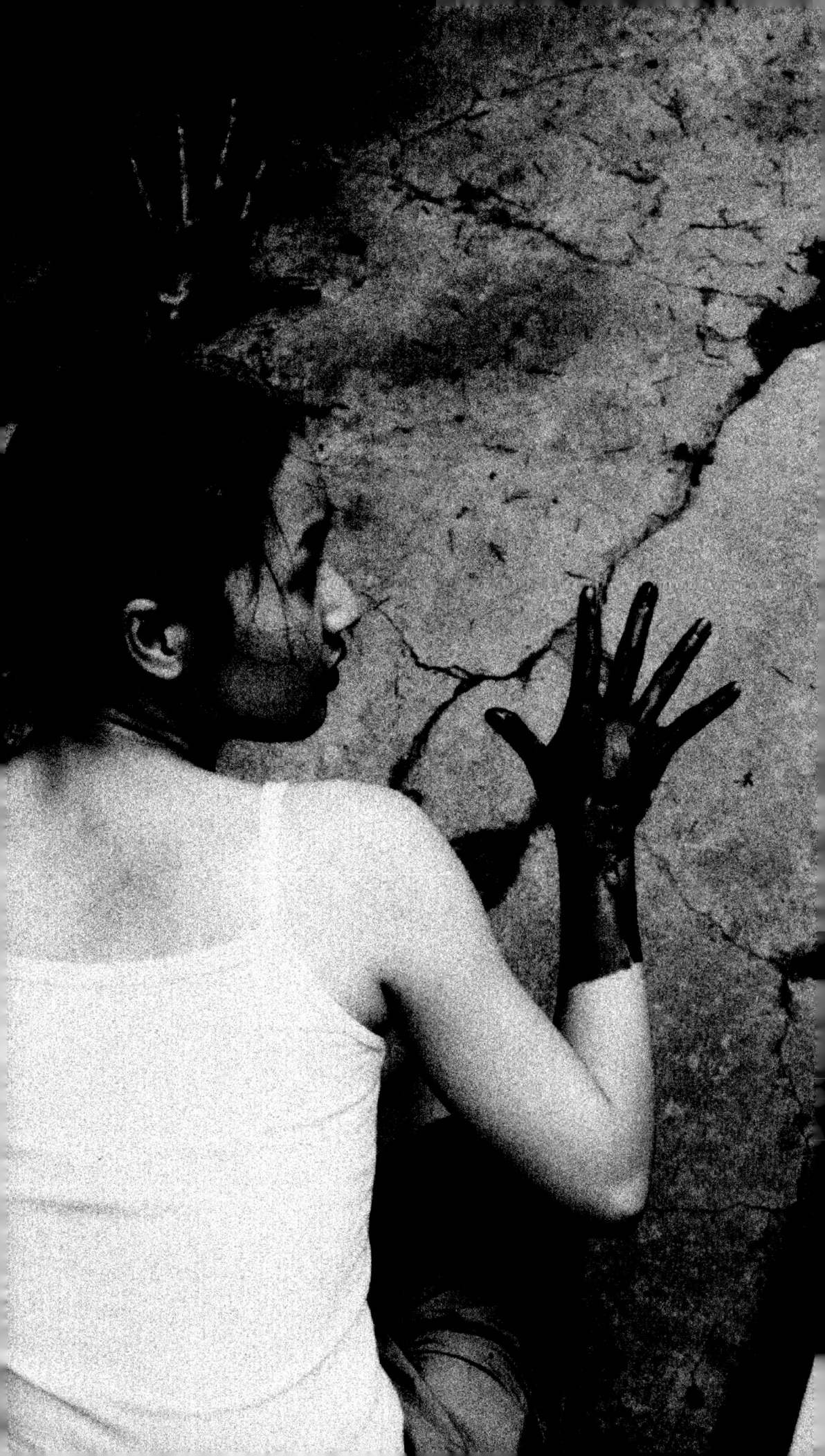

未来的書的未来

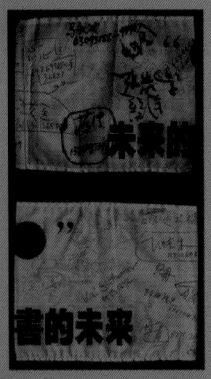

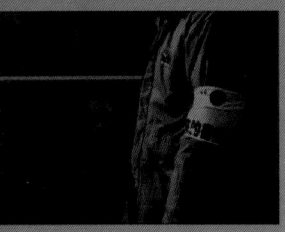

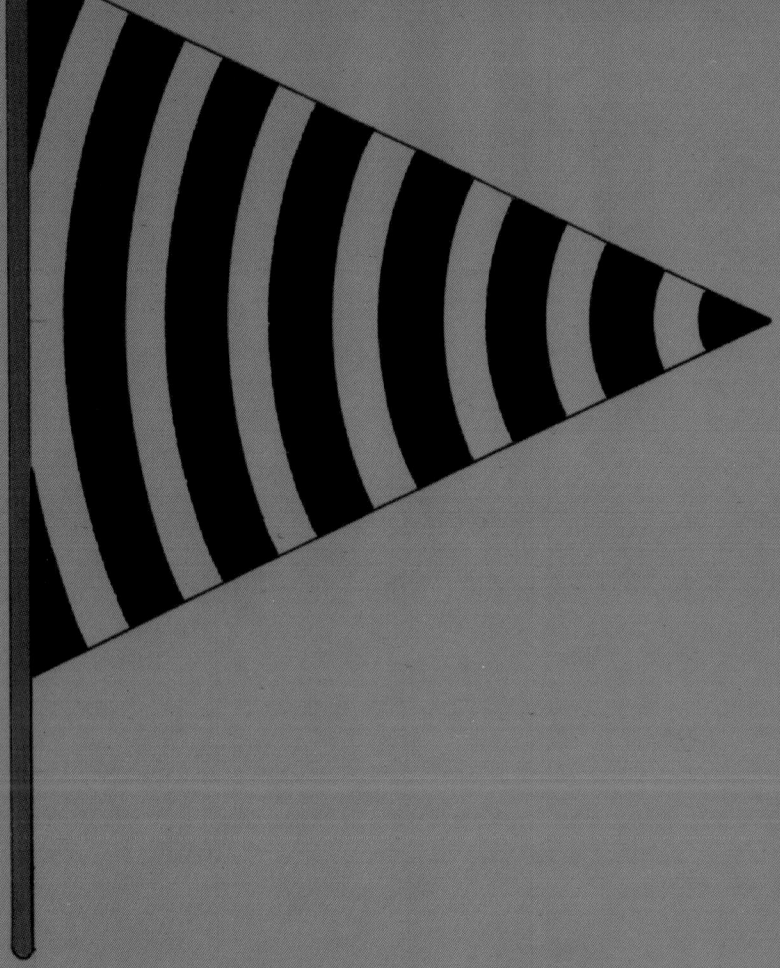

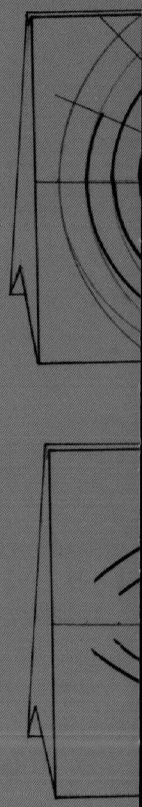

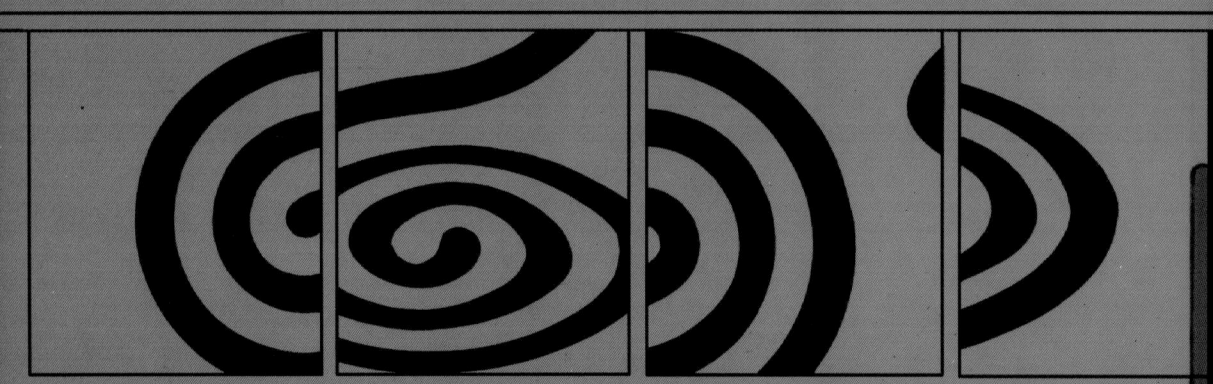

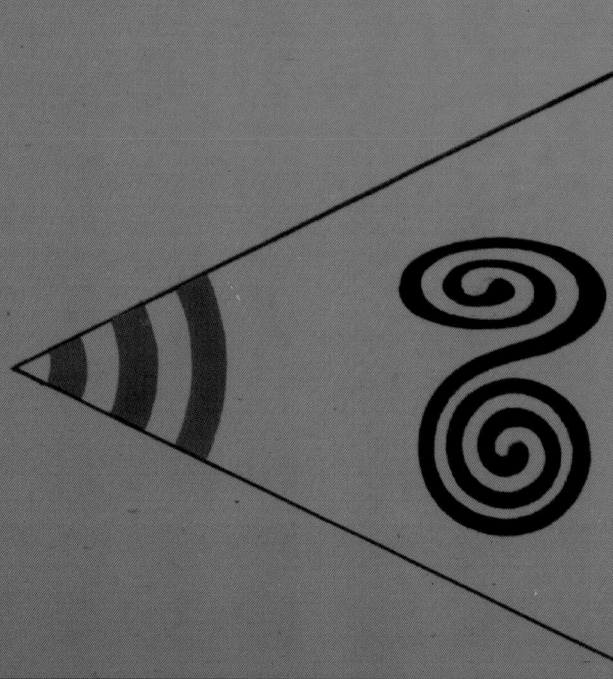

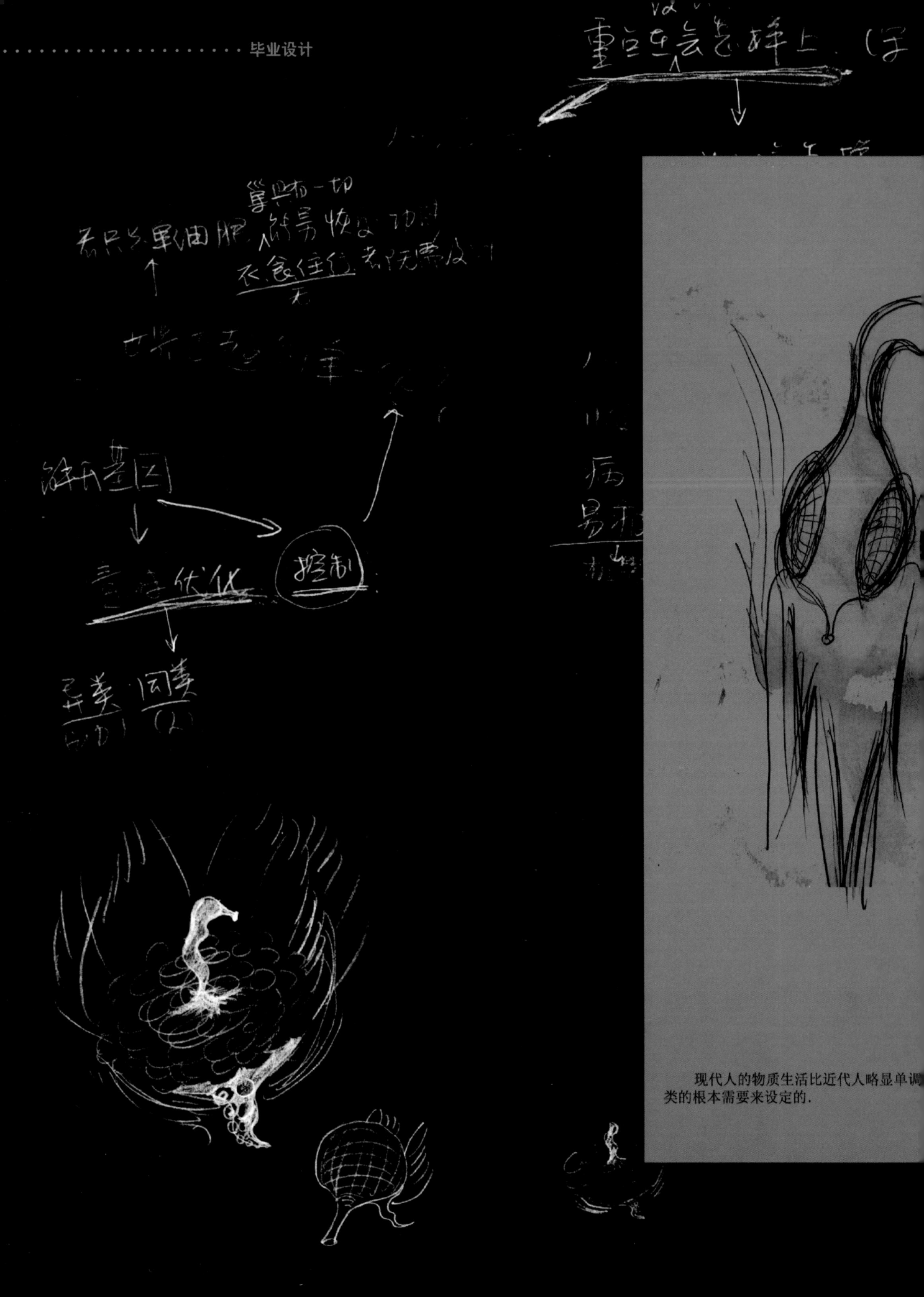

现代人的物质生活比近代人略显单调
类的根本需要来设定的.

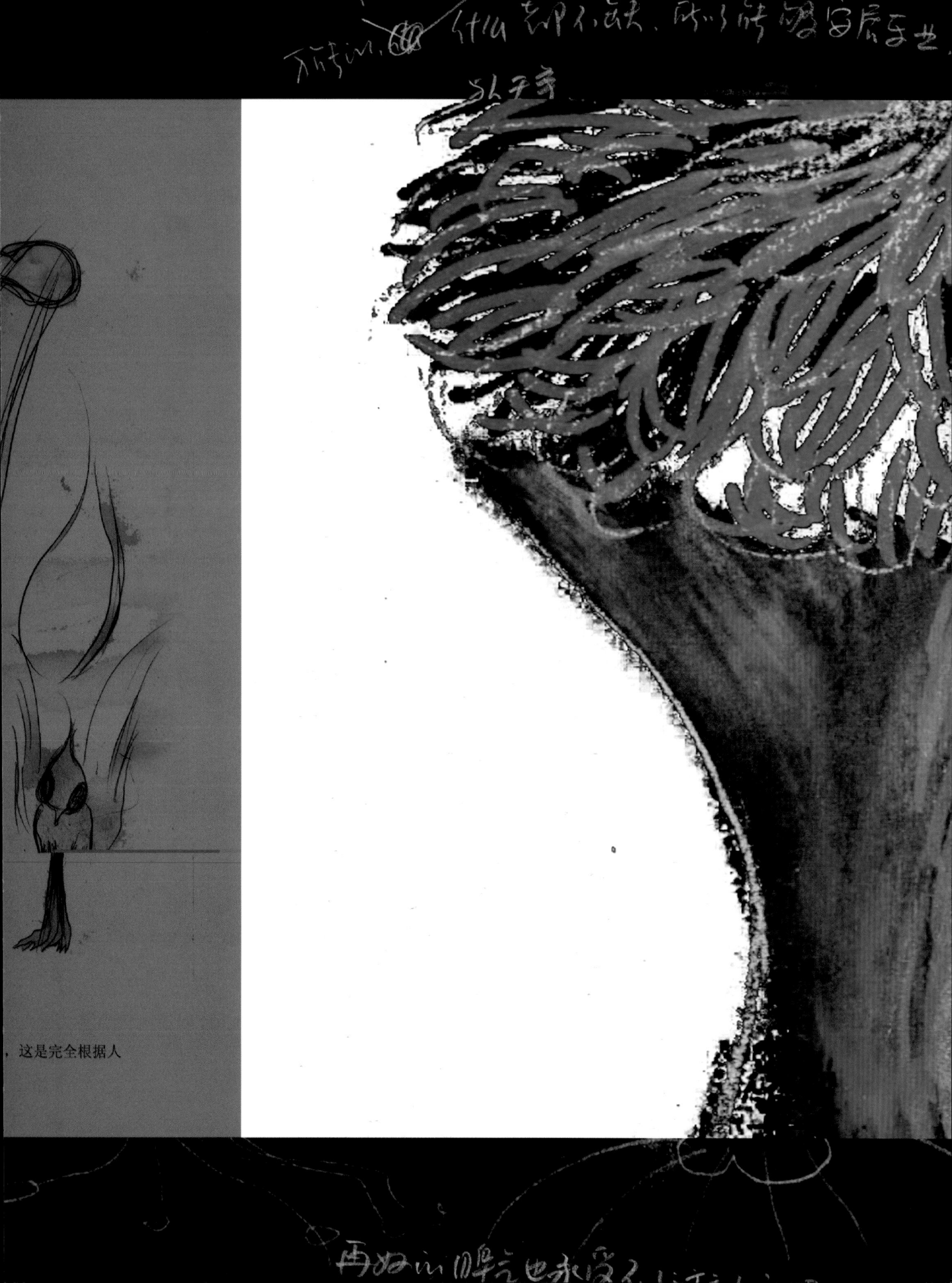

，这是完全根据人

刘 涛

1976 年出生于山西太原

1996 年考入中央美术学院

2000 年毕业于中央美术学院获学士学位

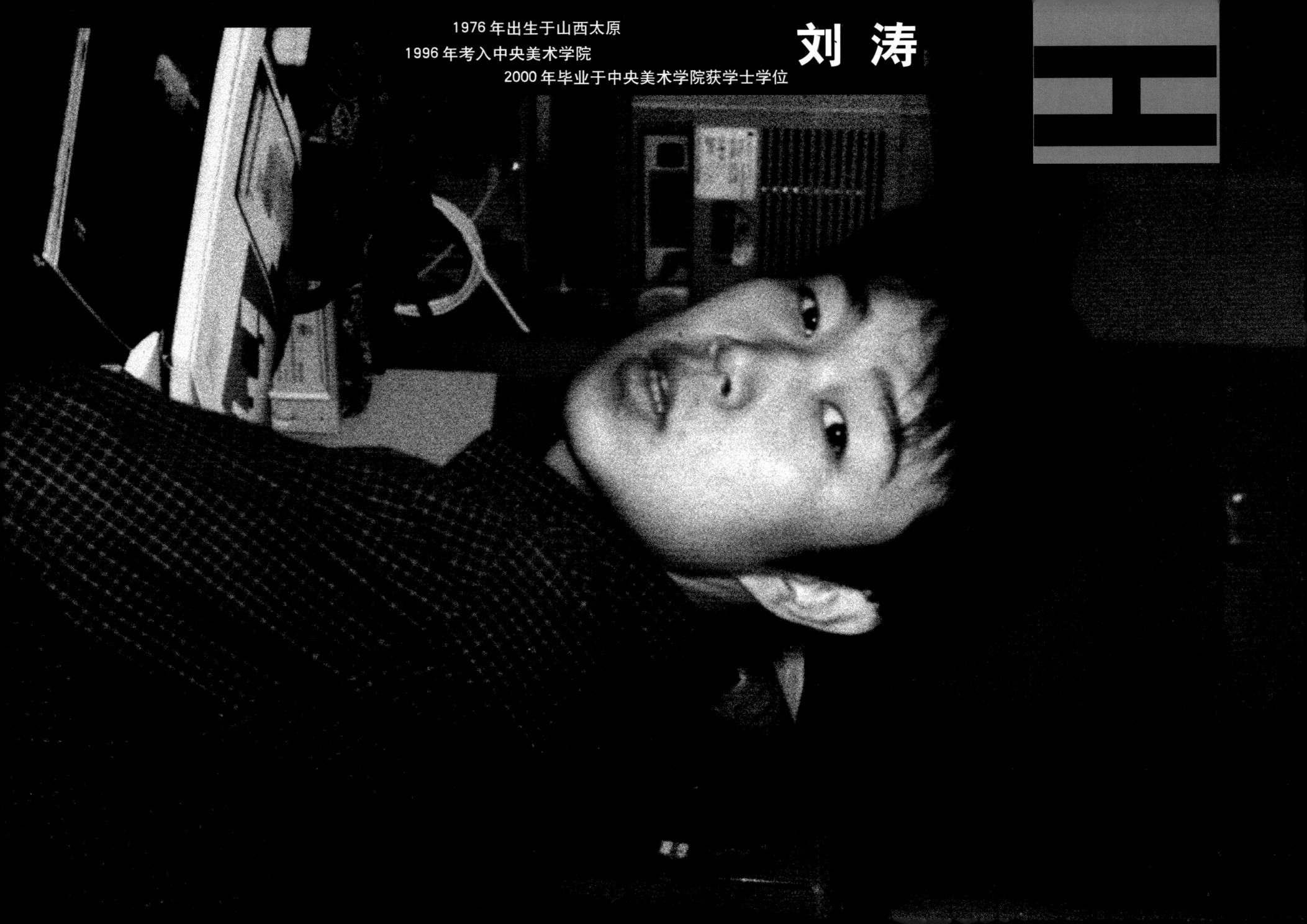

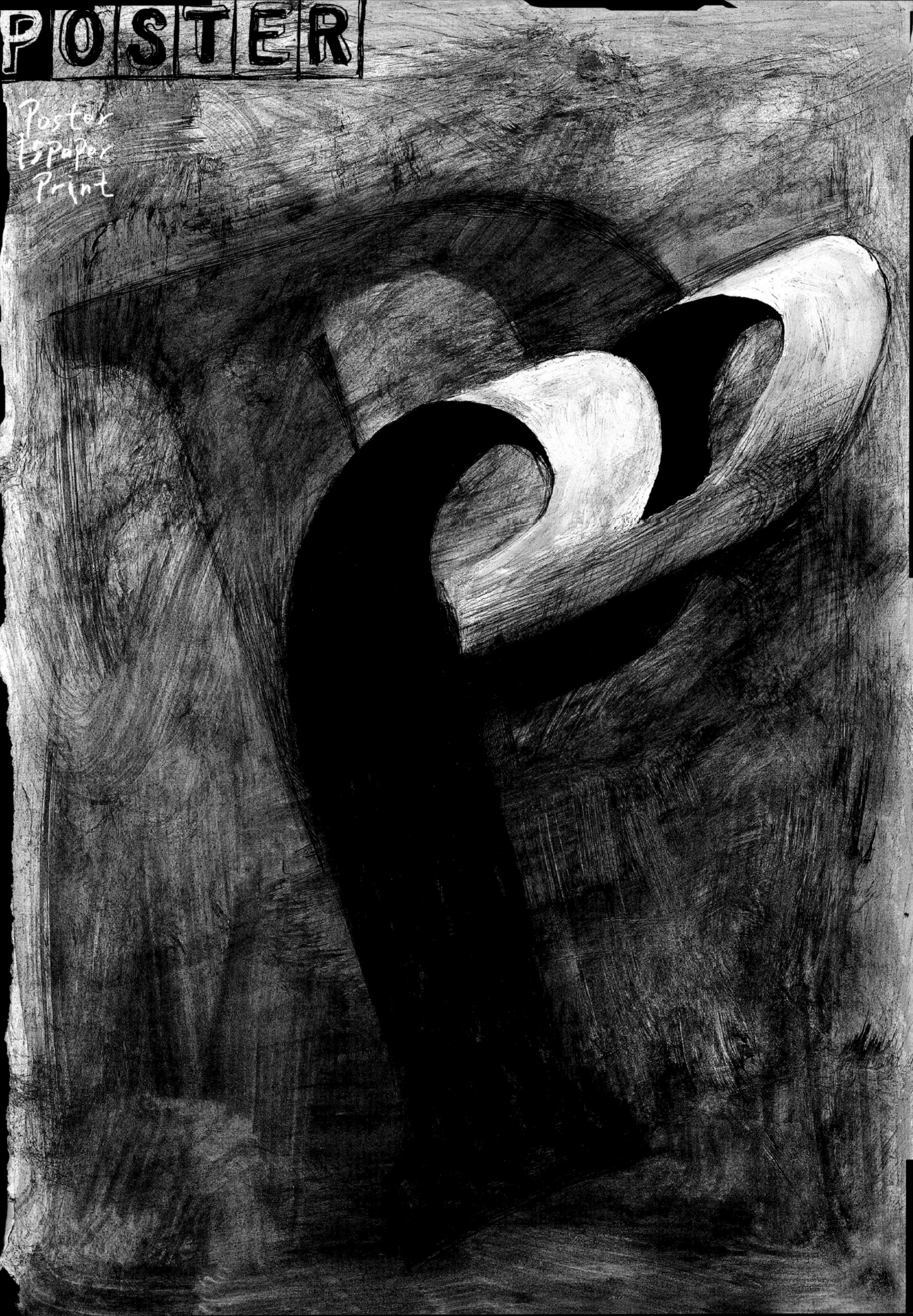
POSTER
Poster
Espaper
Print

POSTER

Poster is organ
Communicate

Poster is
space of contrad-
ictory
exchange
interaction

POSTER

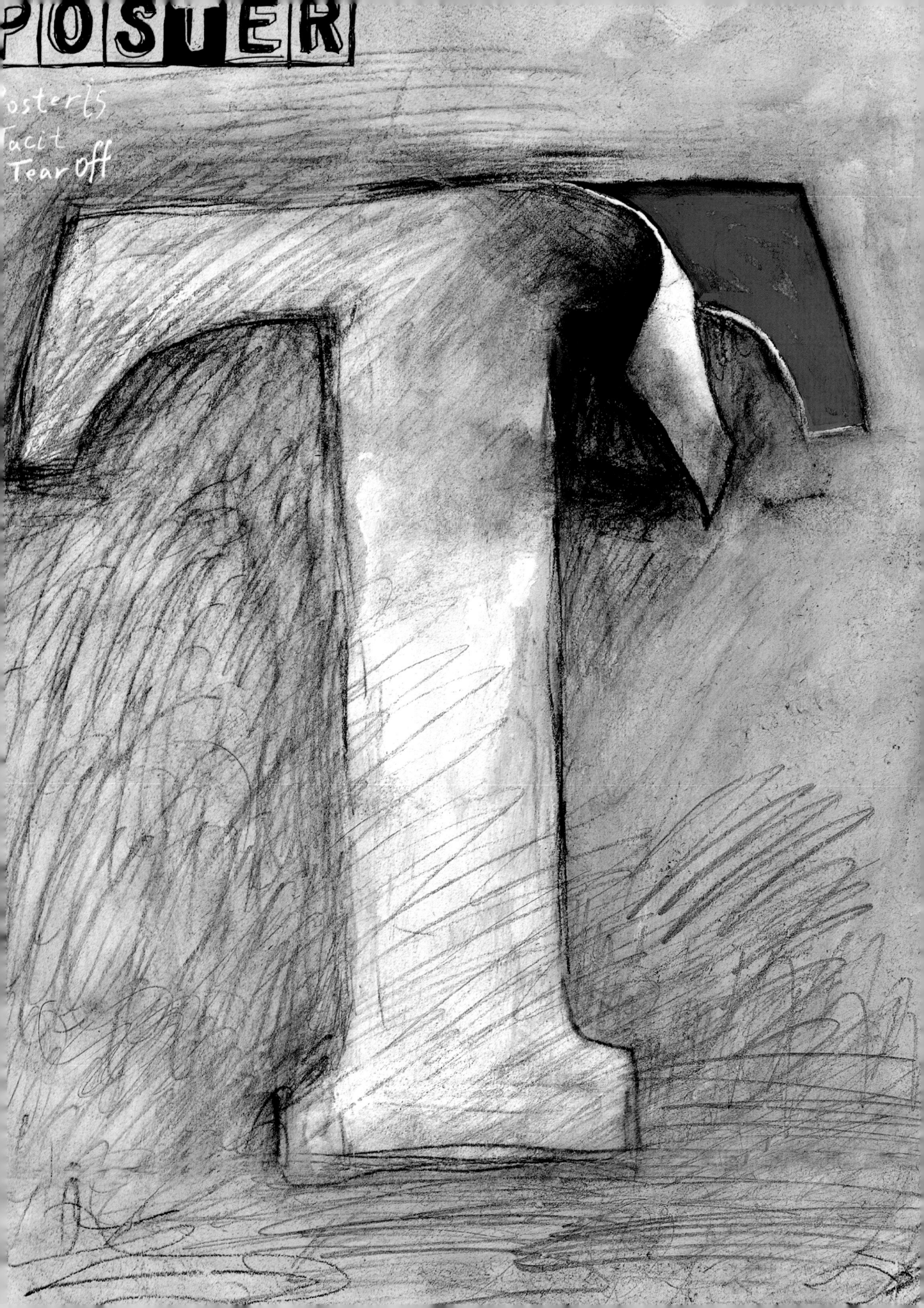
POSTER
Poster/5
Tacit
Tear Off

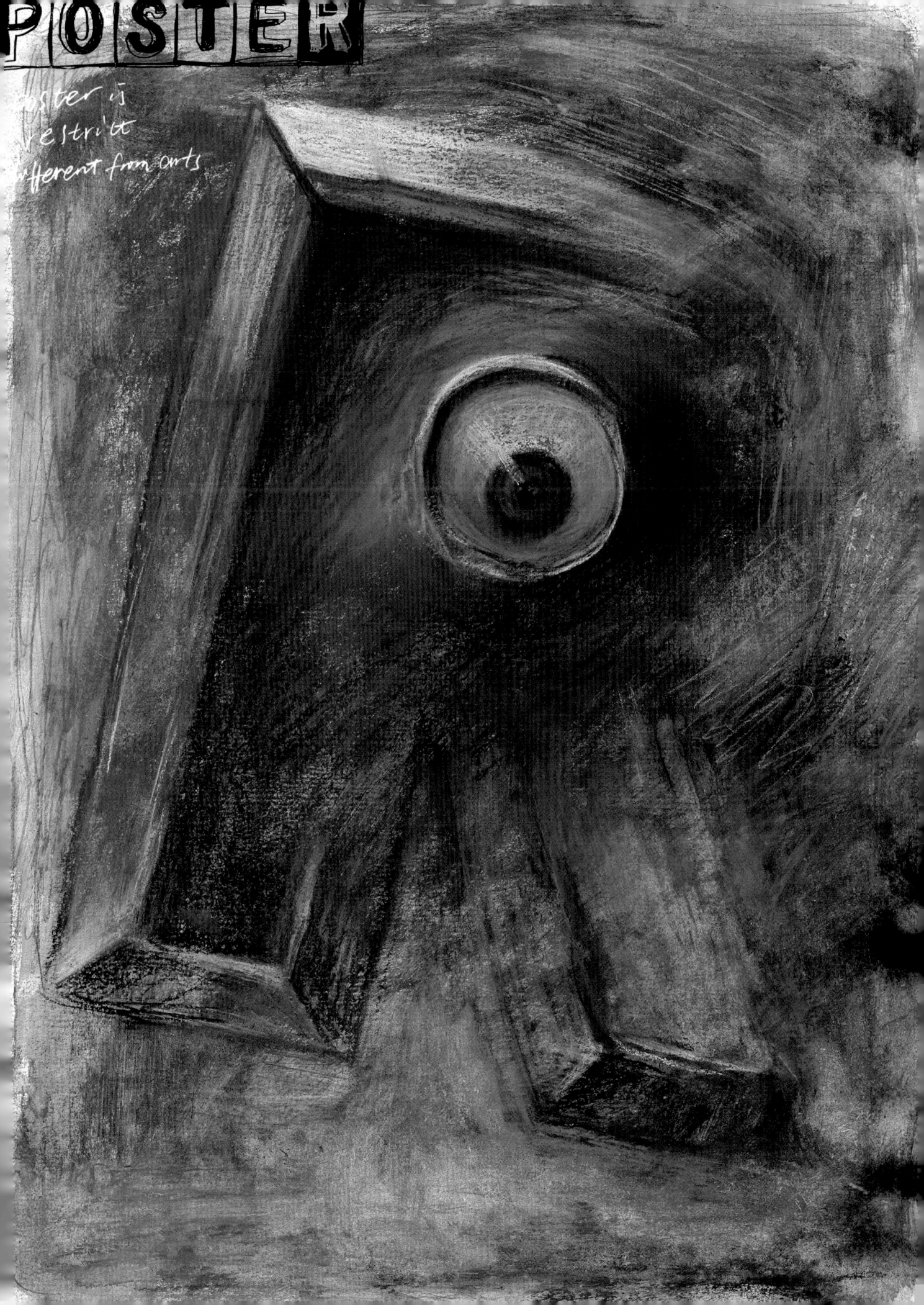
POSTER
oster is
restrict
ifferent from arts

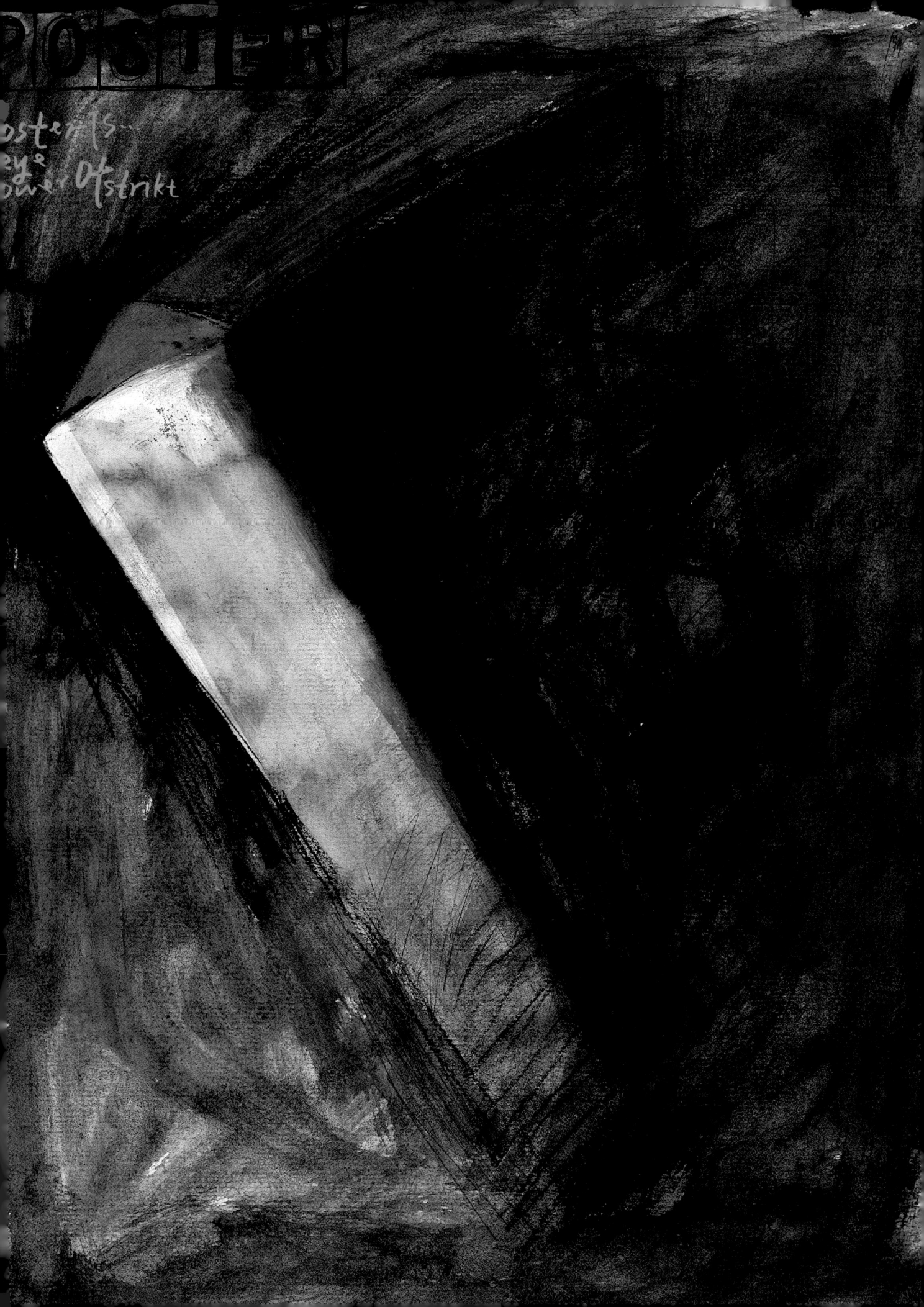
POSTER
osters
ey
ower Of strikt

陈 礼

1973年出生于湖南

997年考入中央美术学院设计系

2001年毕业于中央美术学院获学士学位

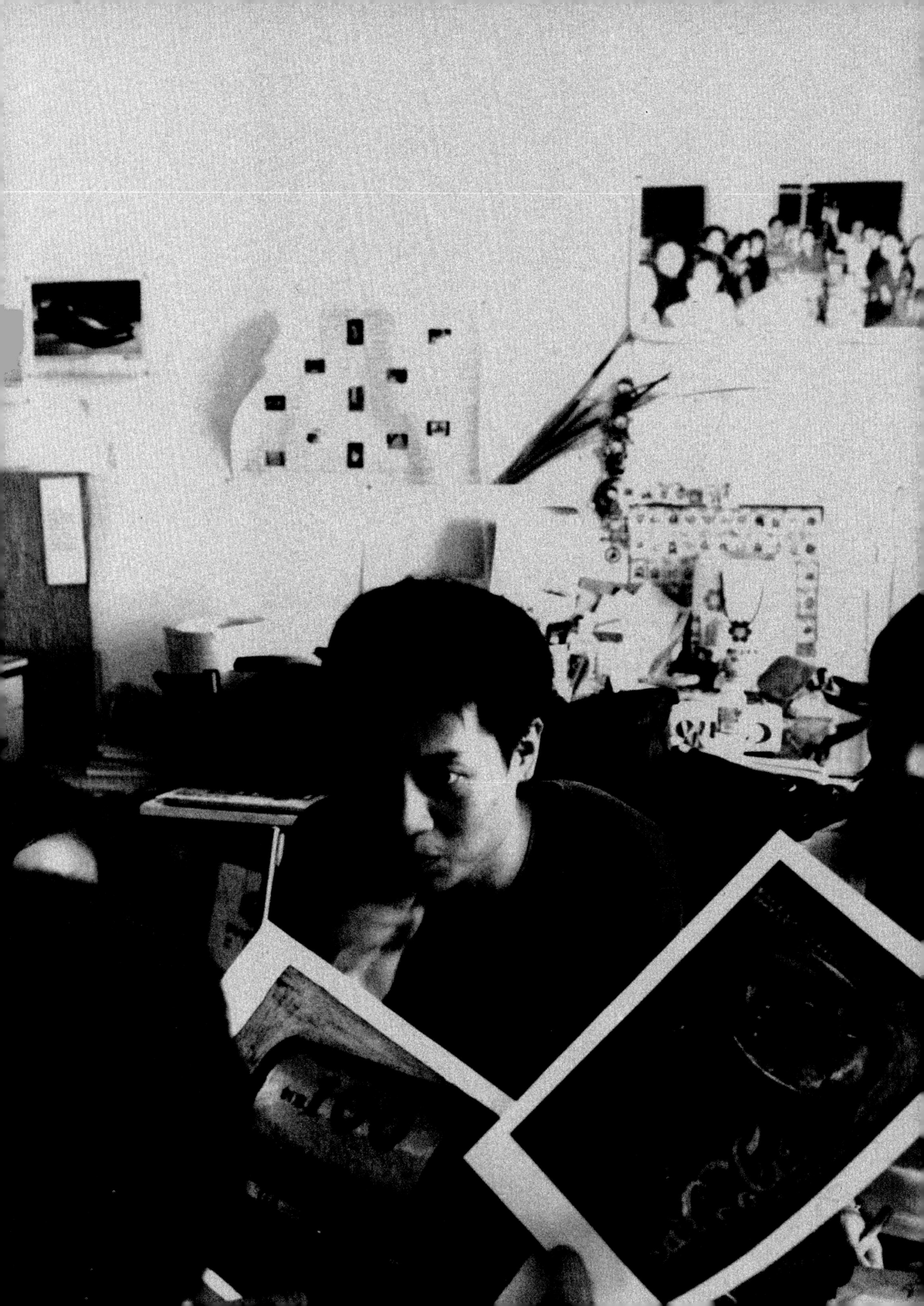

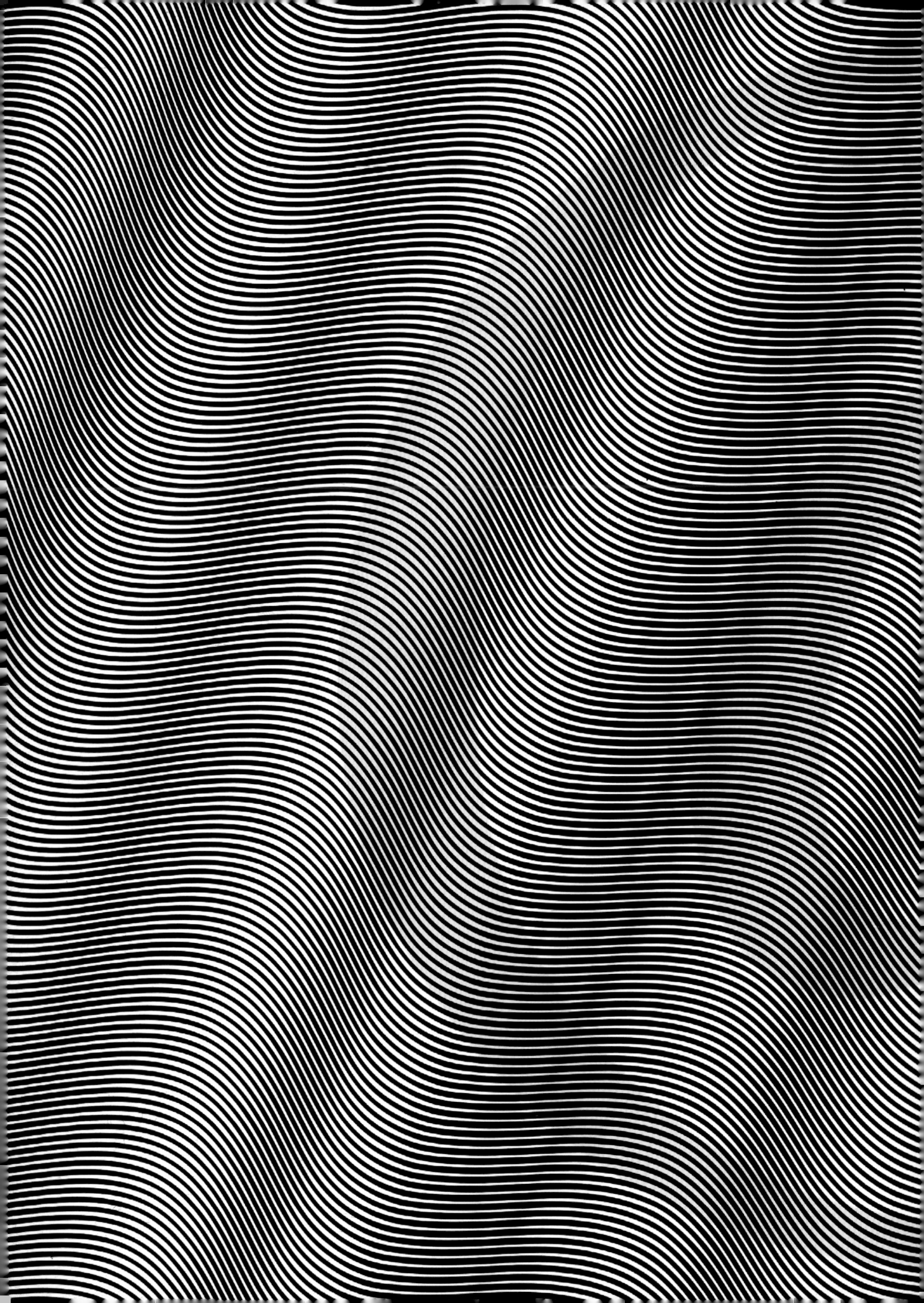

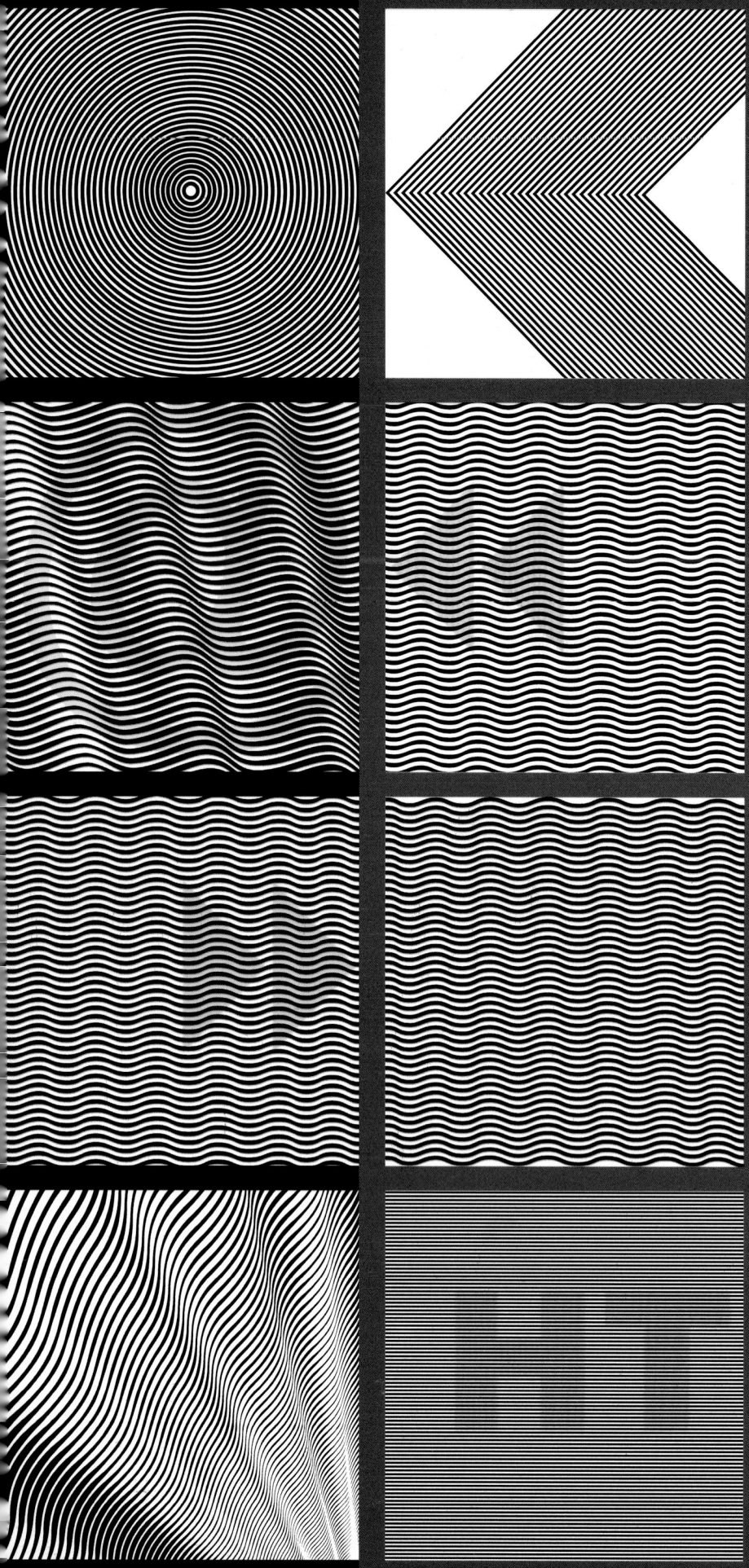

毕业设计

J

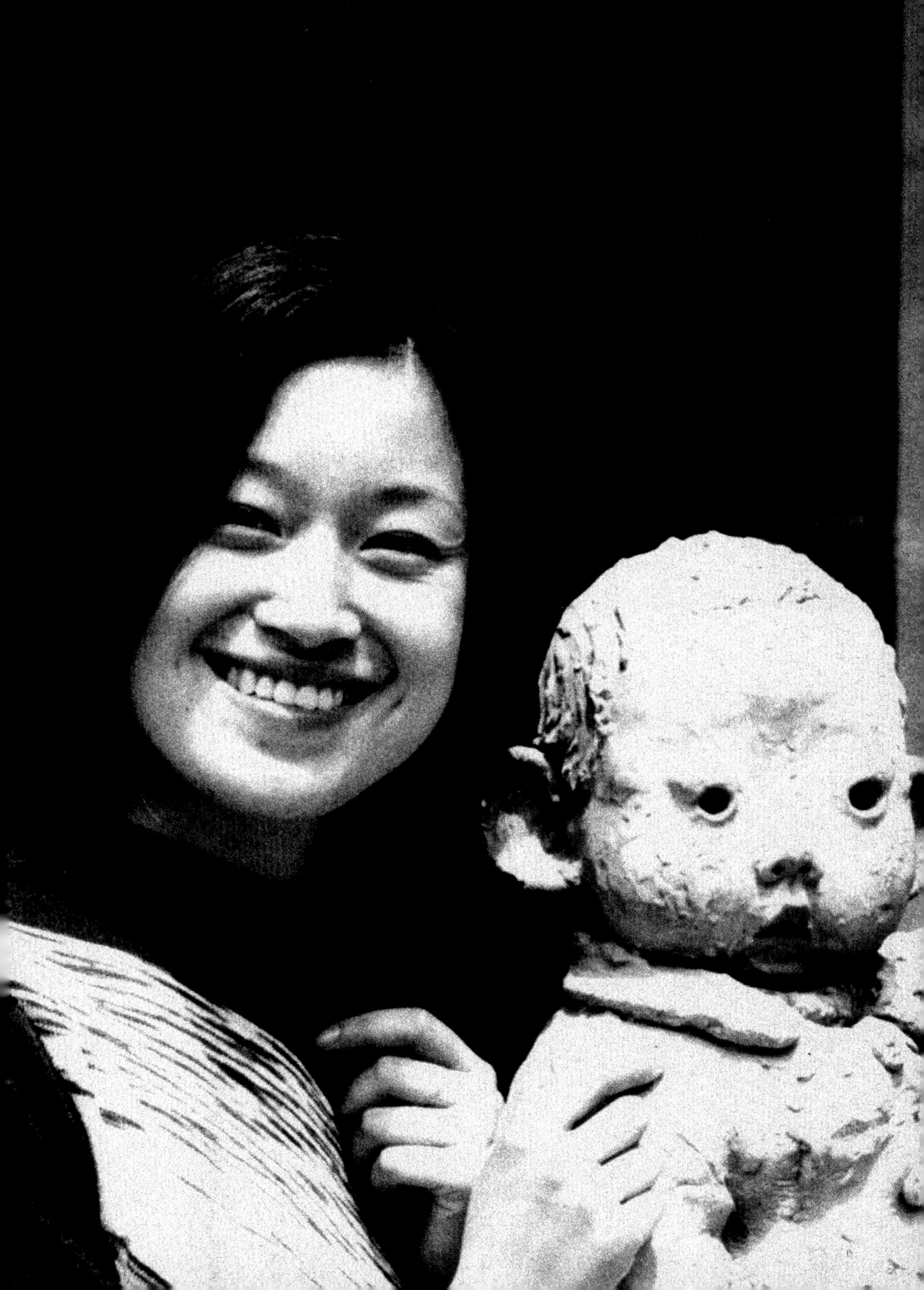

[illegible]

[illegible]

[illegible]

通告

上大樣原是我仏
法和尚想通屋
法所居大法法令所
和尚法所修行我說

76.9.1

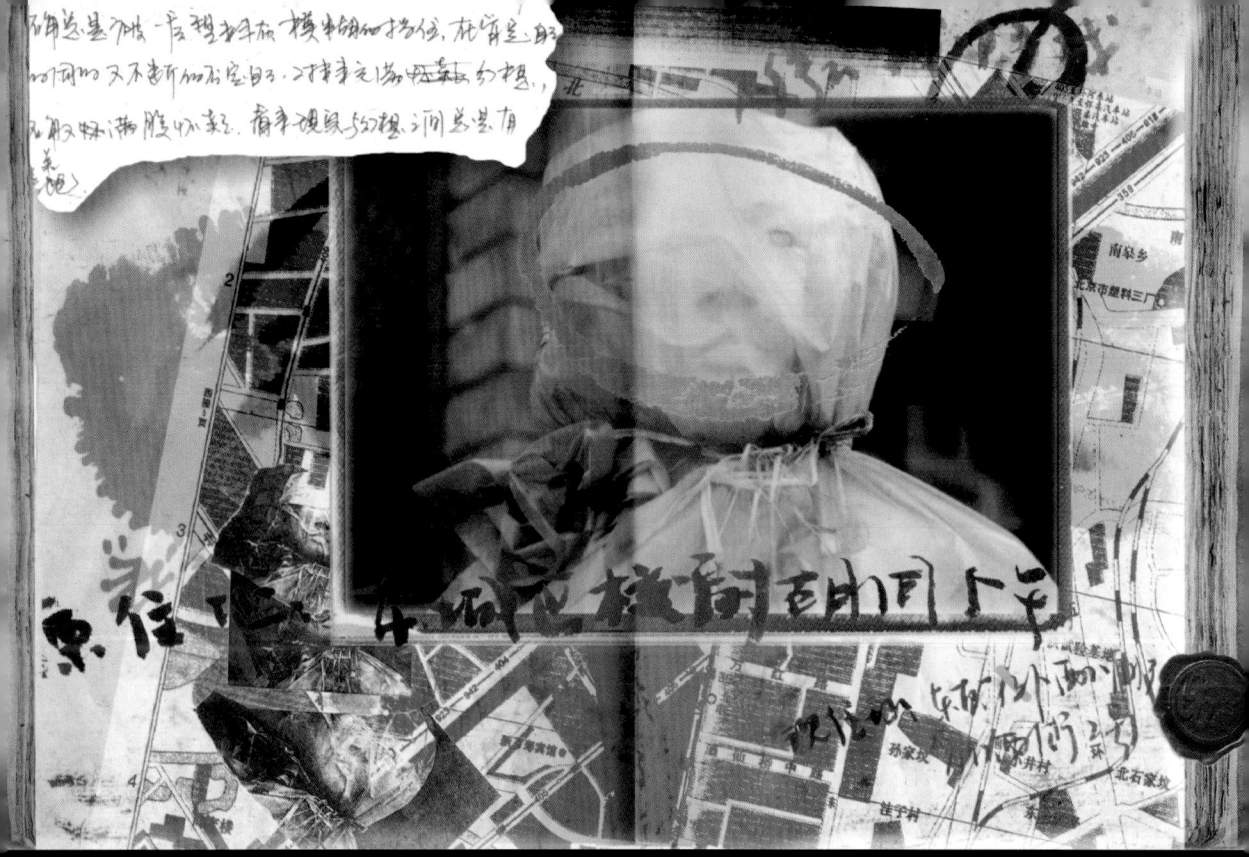
南最乡
北京市燃料三厂
孙家坟
北石家坟
洼宇村

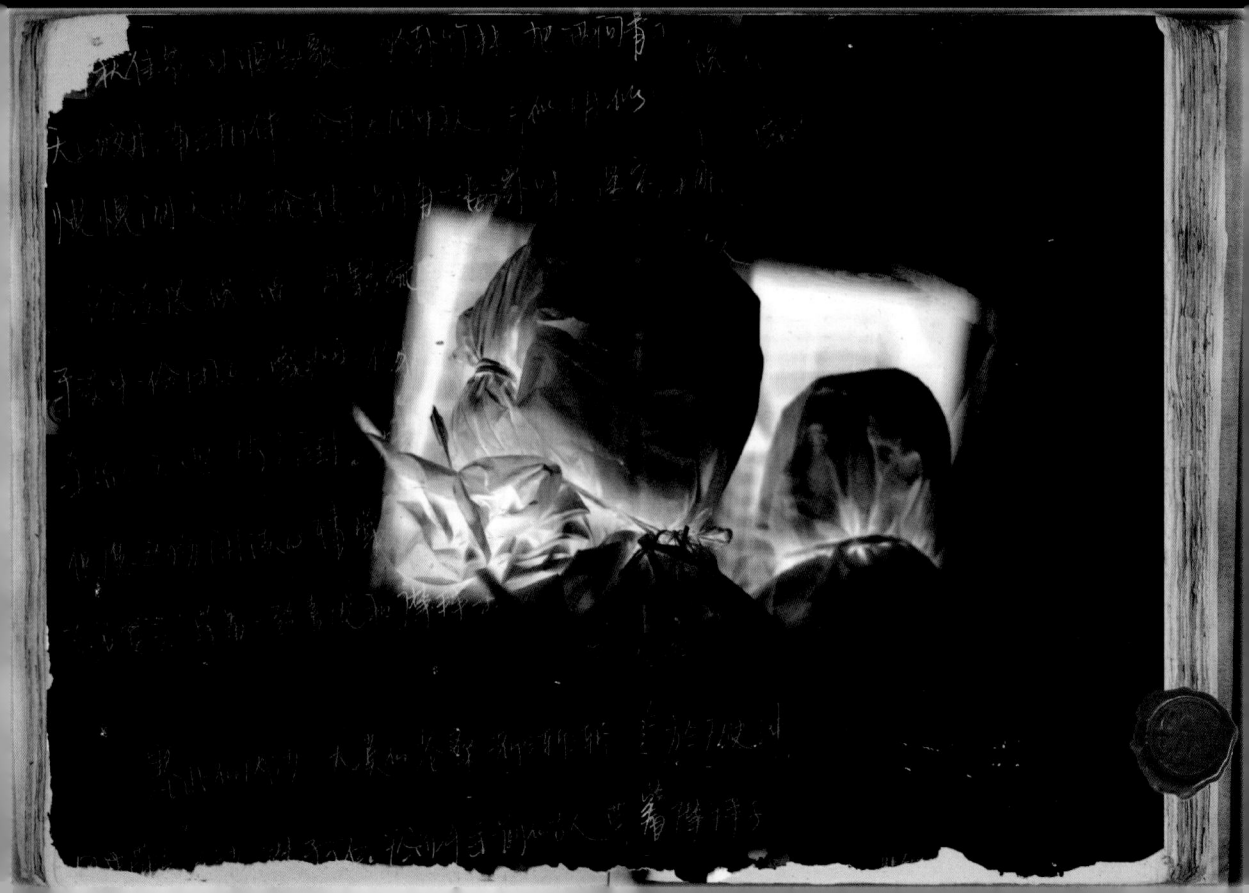

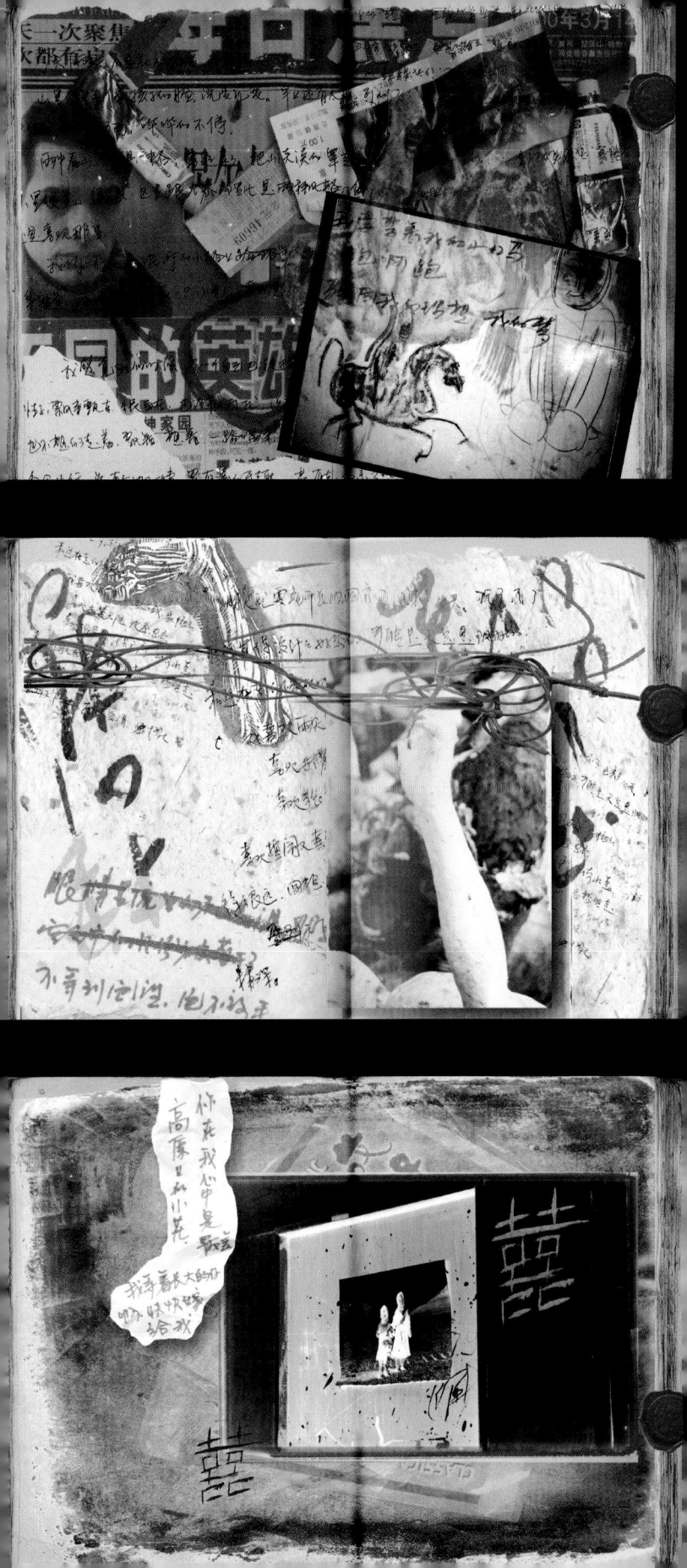
高傲是我小花
我等着长大的你
吧你快快来
冷我
囍
囍

陈曦

1979 年出生于山西太原

1995 年考入中央美术学院附中

1999 年考入中央美术学院设计系

2001 年作品获首届中国平面设计大赛优秀奖

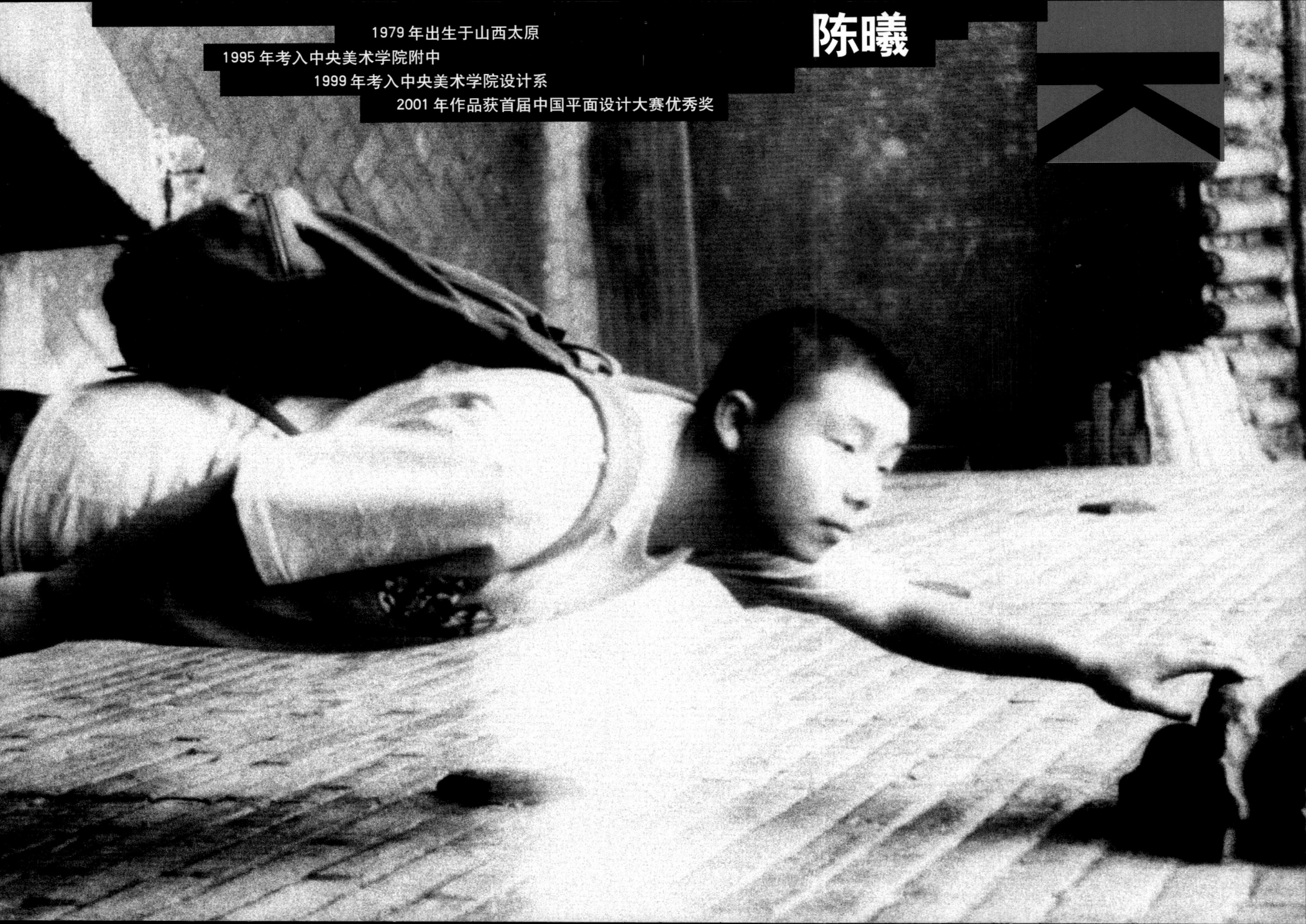

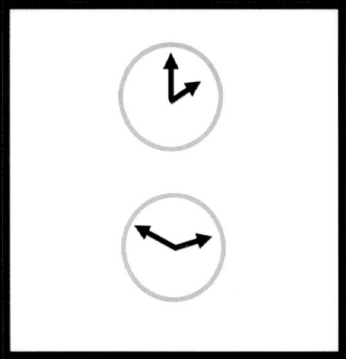

时间

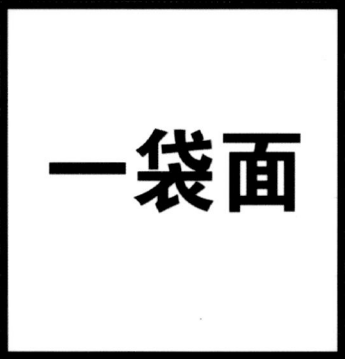

重量

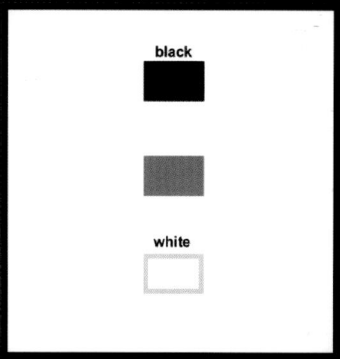

浓度

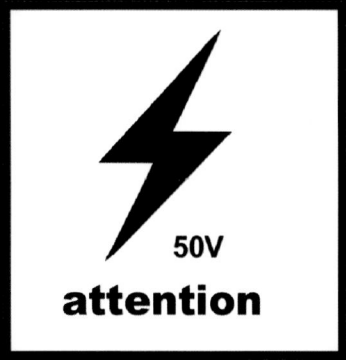

电压

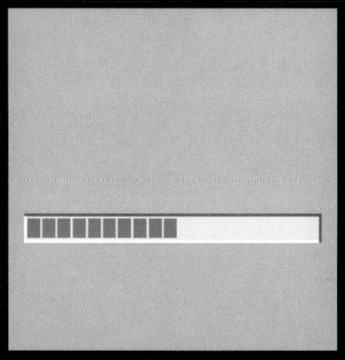

进度

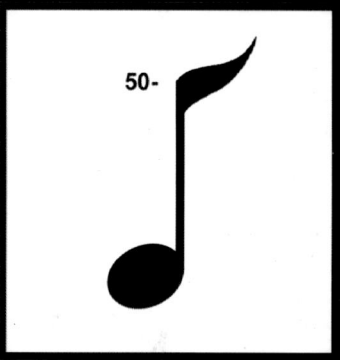

五十分音符

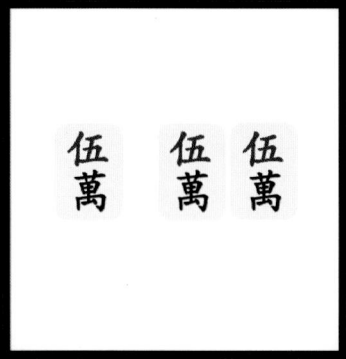

“禄”

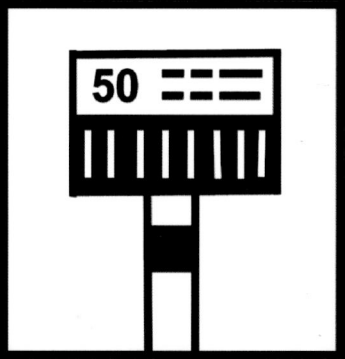

站牌

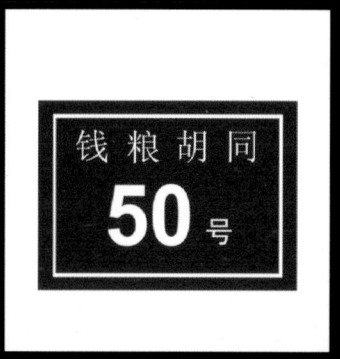

门牌

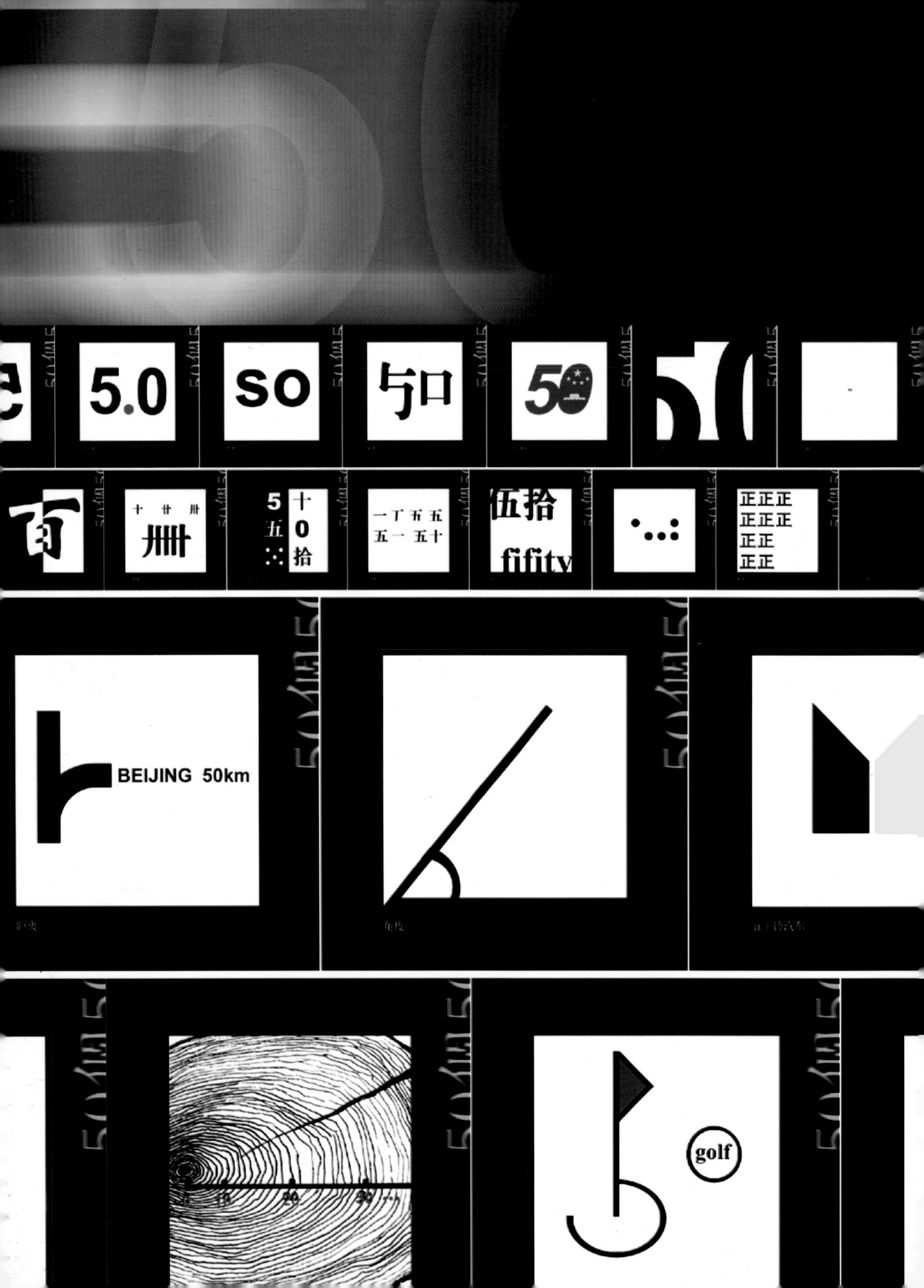
5.0
so
与口
50
百
十 廿 卅
卌
5 十
五 0
拾
一丁五五
五一五十
伍拾
fifity
正正正
正正正
正正
正正
BEIJING 50km
golf

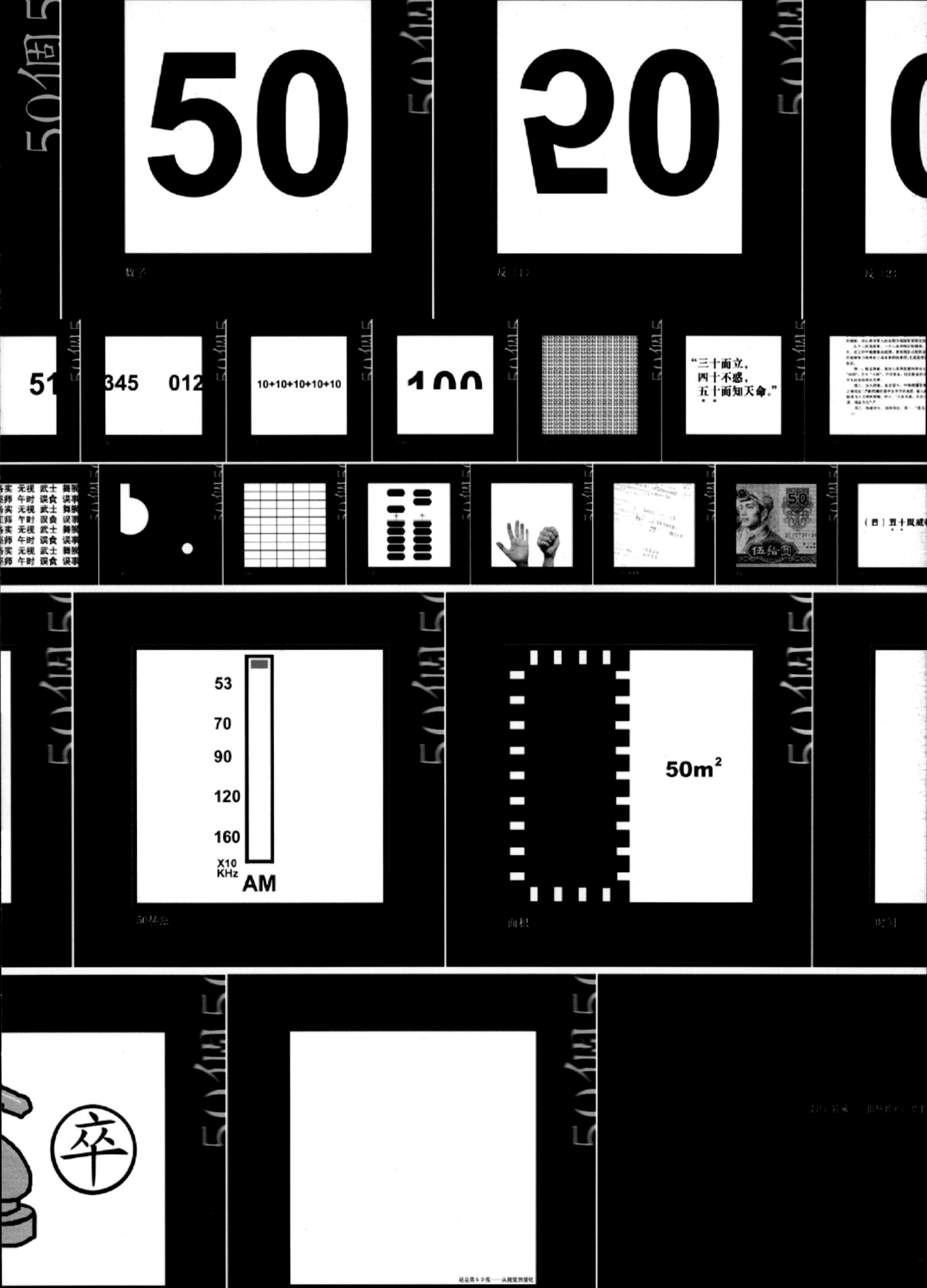
50个圆
50
数字
20
反（1）
反（2）
51
345 012
10+10+10+10+10
100
“三十而立，
四十不感，
五十而知天命。”
（四）五十周威
53
70
90
120
160
X10
KHz
AM
50m²
面积
卒

Fine Arts

The Central academy of Fine Arts

Design Dept.

100015

197 9cx@sina.com

95950-2636 550

64319589

chenxi

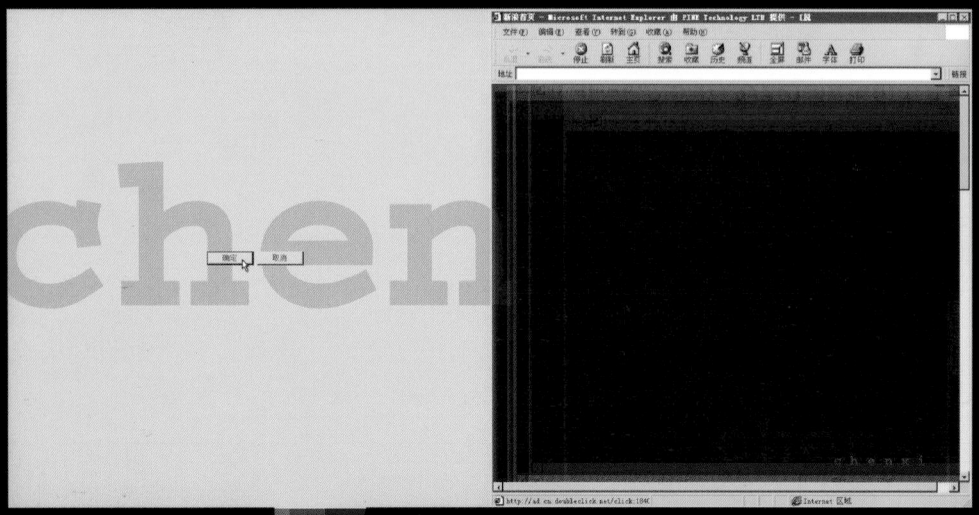

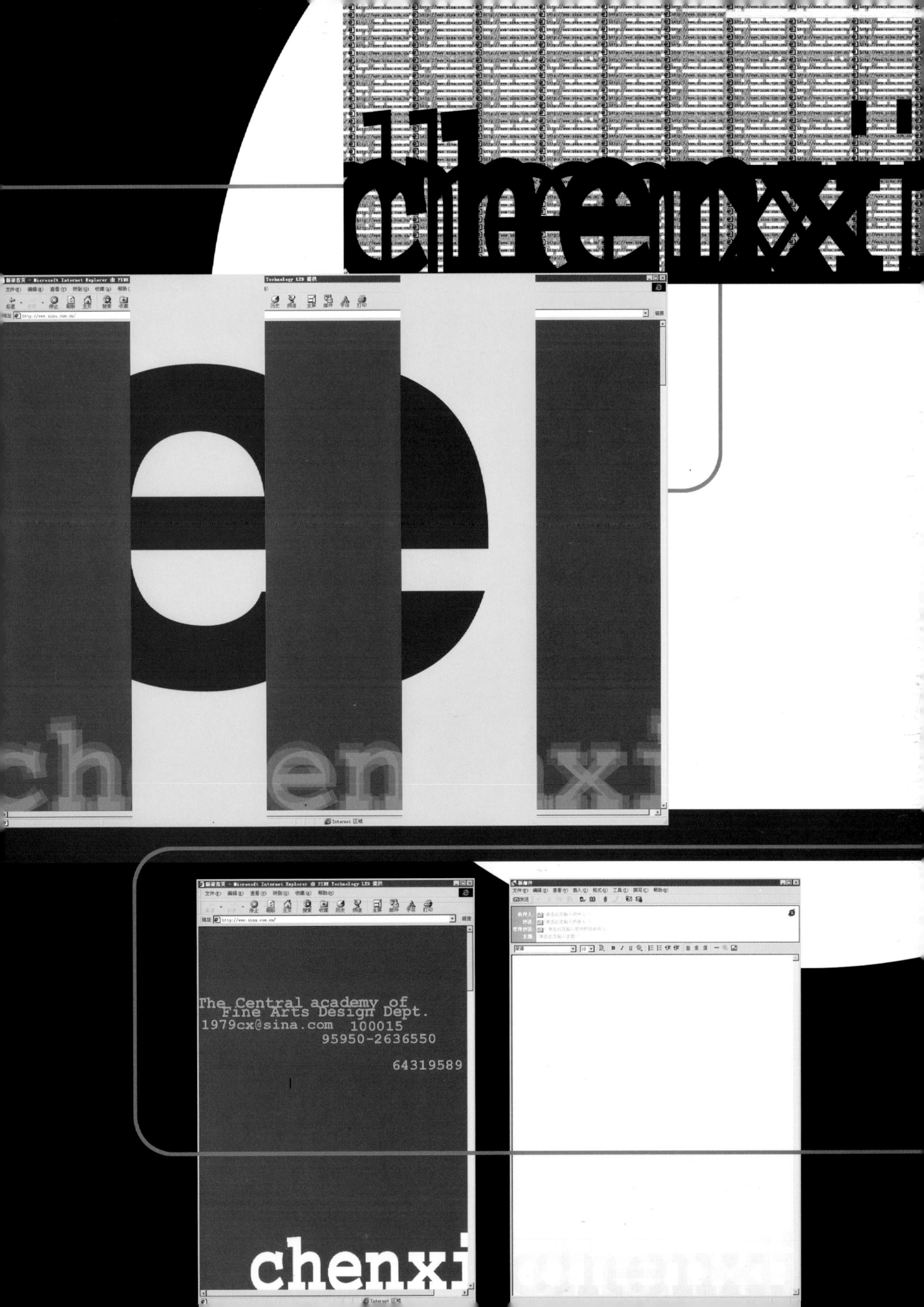
The Central academy of
Fine Arts Design Dept.
1979cx@sina.com 100015
95950-2636550
64319589
chenxi

徐光东

1973 年出生于辽宁省抚顺市
1993 年毕业于抚顺艺专美术专业
1999 年毕业于中央美术学院设计系获学士学位
现任教于北京市工艺美术学校平面设计专业
同时任职金马广告有限公司·北京分公司创作总监

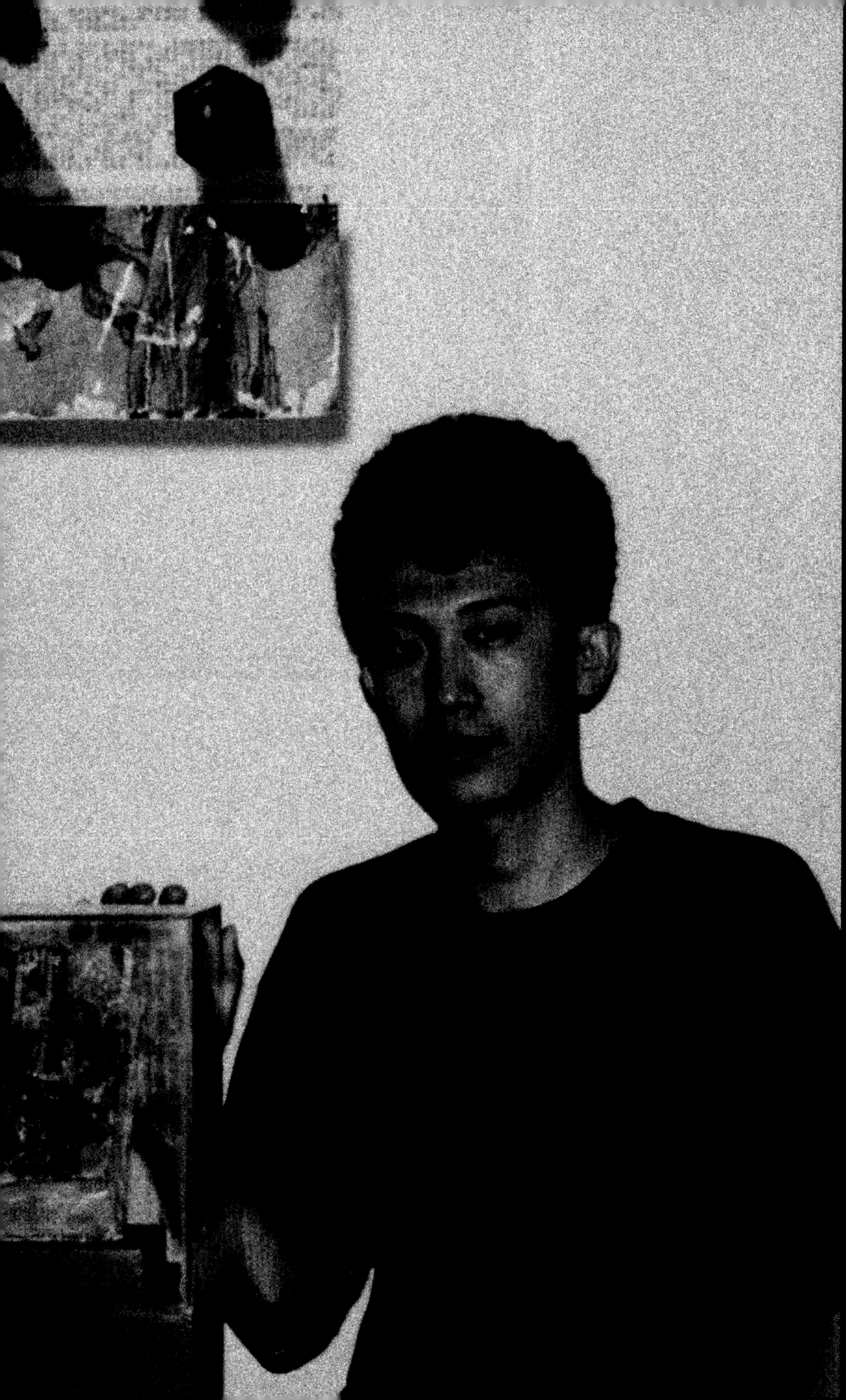

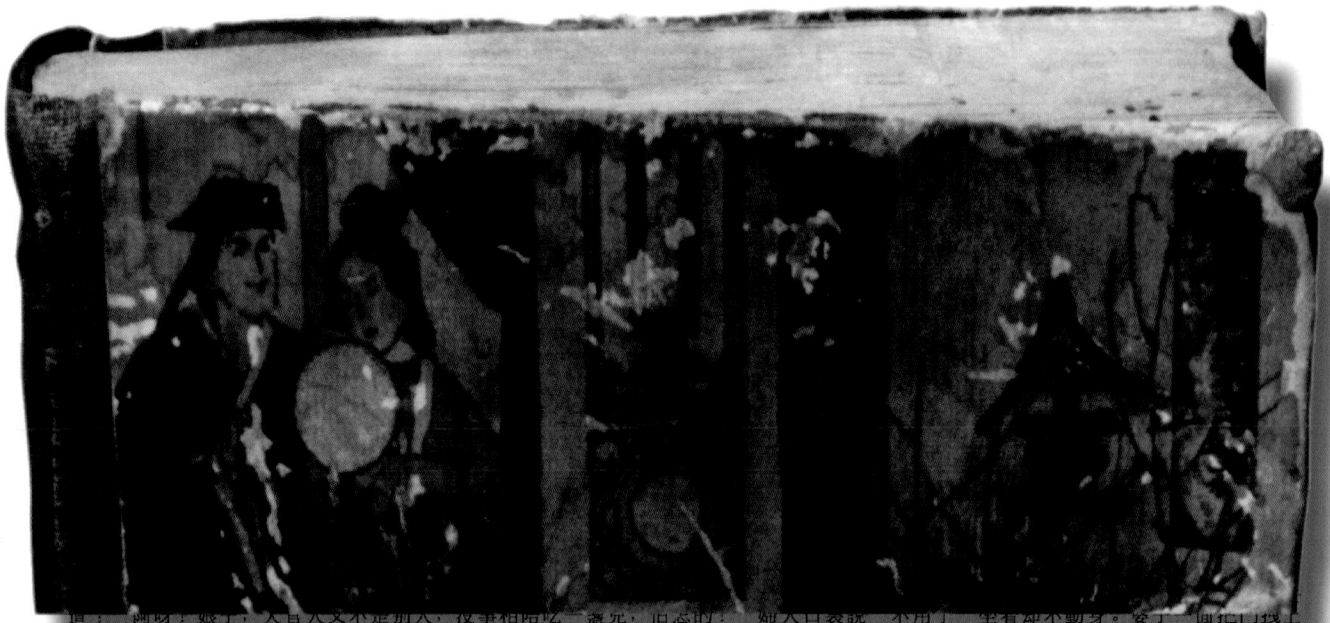

在屋裏。當路坐了，一頭續着鎖。

婆去了，倒把椅兒扯開一邊坐着，却衹偷眼睃看。西門慶坐在對面，一徑把那雙涎瞪瞪的眼睛看着他，便又問道：“却才到忘了問

帶笑的回道：“姓武。”西門慶故做不聽得，說道：“姓堵？”那婦人却把頭又別轉着，笑

是姓武。衹是俺清河縣妳

“便是奴的丈夫。

慶道：“我替娘子

斜溜他一眼兒。

着袖兒別轉着，

上去，却故意把

，讓他吃菜兒。

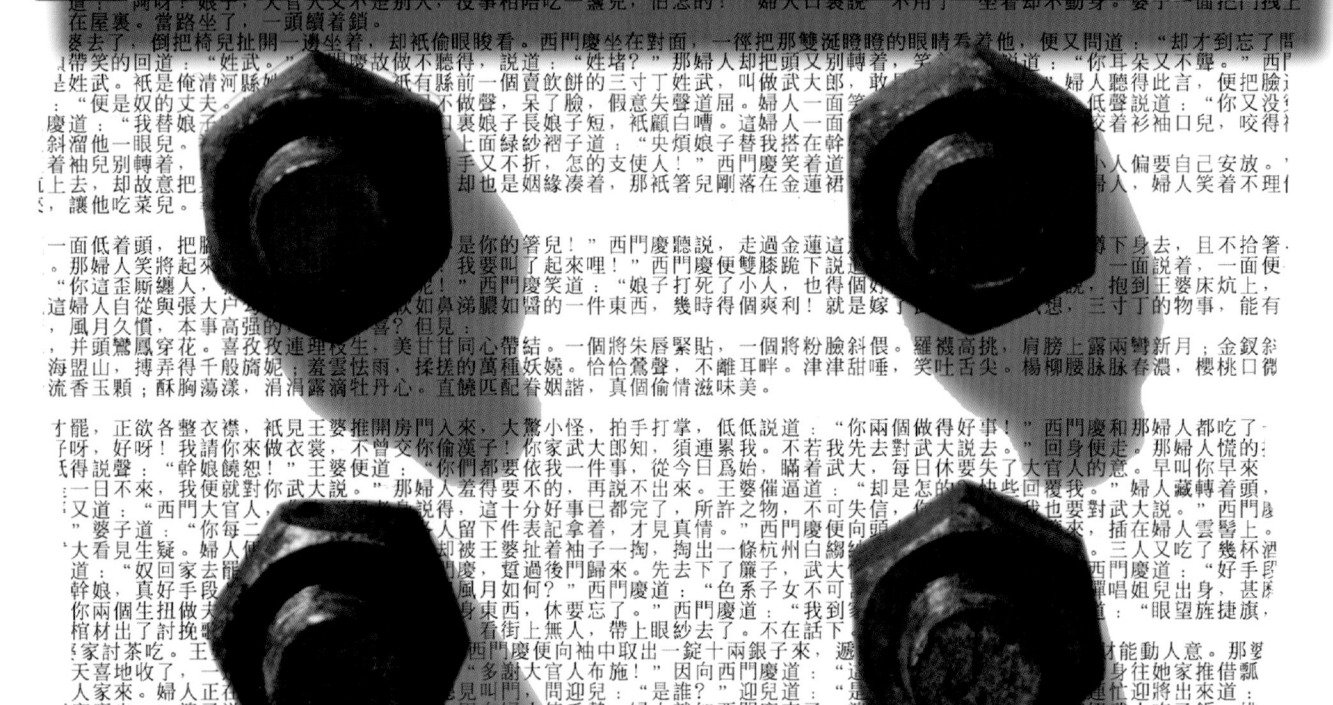

一面低着頭，把

。那婦人笑將起來

“你這歪厮纏人，

這婦人自從與張大户

，風月久慣，本事高强的

，并頭鸞鳳穿花。喜孜孜連理枝生，美甘甘同心帶結。一個將朱唇緊貼，一個將粉臉斜偎。羅襪高挑，肩膀上露兩彎新月；金釵斜

海盟山，搏弄得千般旖旎；羞雲怯雨，揉搓的萬種妖嬈。恰恰鶯聲，不離耳畔。津津甜唾，笑吐舌尖。楊柳腰脉脉春濃，櫻桃口微

流香玉顆；酥胸蕩漾，涓涓露滴牡丹心。直饒匹配着姻諧，真個偷情滋味美。

才罷，正欲各整衣襟，衹見王婆推開房門入來，大驚小怪，拍手打掌，低低說道：“你兩個做得好事！”西門慶和那婦人都吃了

子呀，好呀！我請你來做衣裳，不曾交你偷漢子！你家武大郎知，須連累我。不若我先去對武大說去。”回身便走。那婦人慌的

我得說聲：“幹娘饒恕！”王婆便道：“你們都要依我一件事，從今日爲始，瞞着武大，每日休要失了大官人的意。早叫你早來

一日不來，我便就對你武大說。”那婦人羞得要不的，再說不出來。王婆催逼道：“却是怎的，快些回覆我。”婦人藏轉着頭，

又道：“西門大官人，

”婆子道：“你每二

大看見生疑。婦人

道：“奴回家去罷

幹娘，真好手段

你兩個生扭做夫

棺材出了討挽

家討茶吃。王

天喜地收了，

人家來。婦人正在

家裏坐。”婆子道

換了一套艷色新衣，

王婆茶坊裏來。正是：

笑，心裏原來别有仁。有詞單道這雙關二意：　這瓢是瓢，口兒小身子兒大。你幼在春風棚上恁兒高，到大來人難要。他今

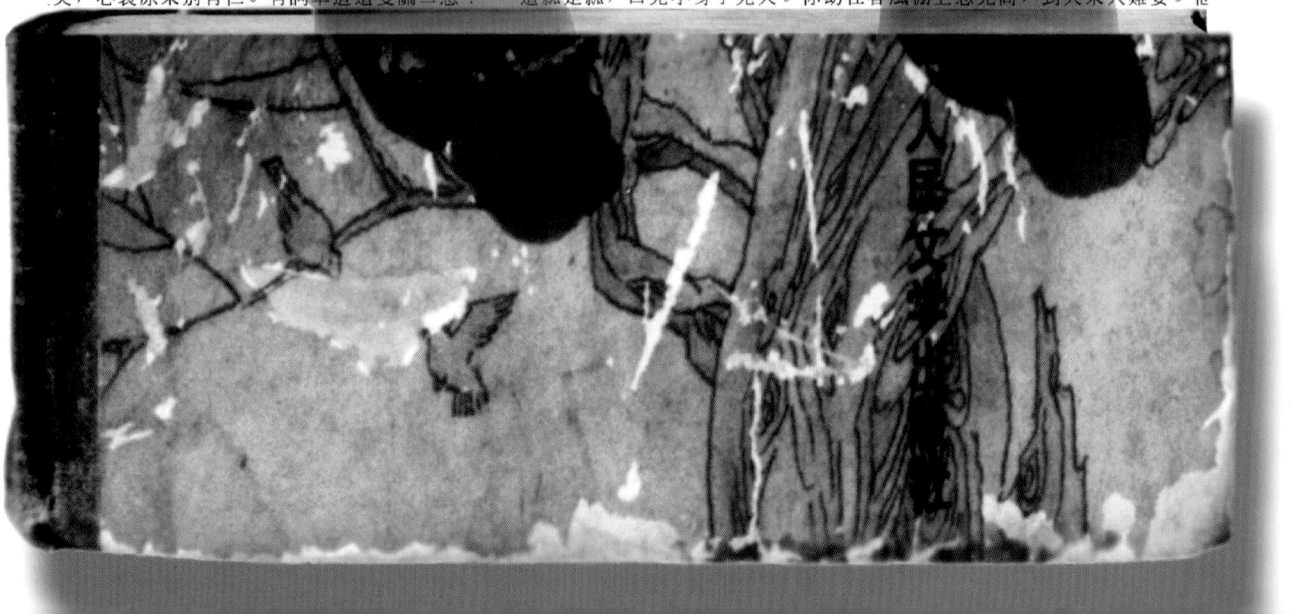

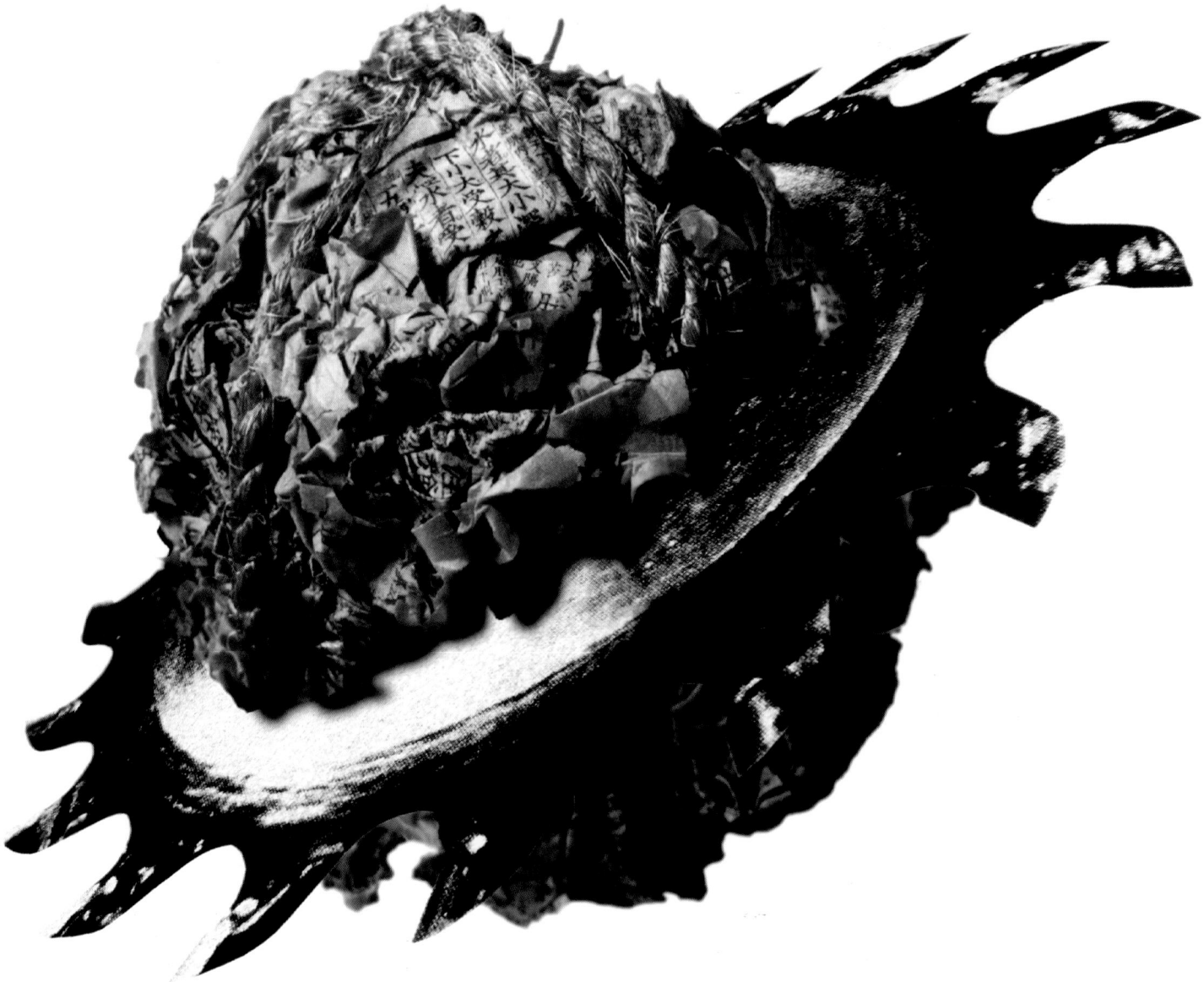

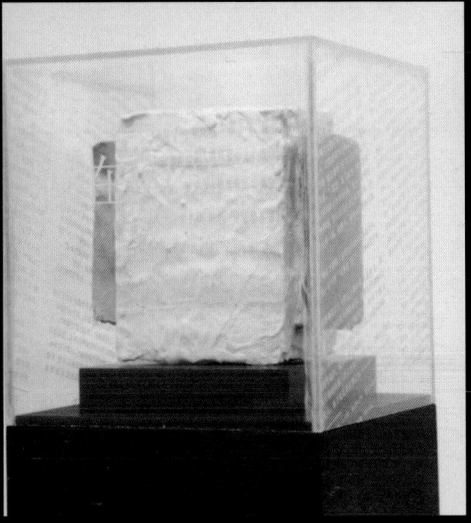

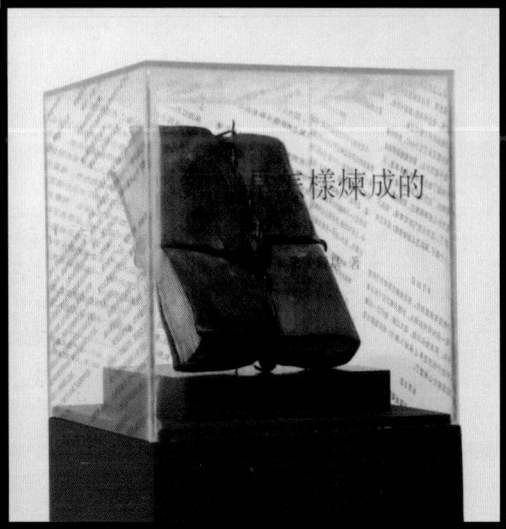
樣煉成的

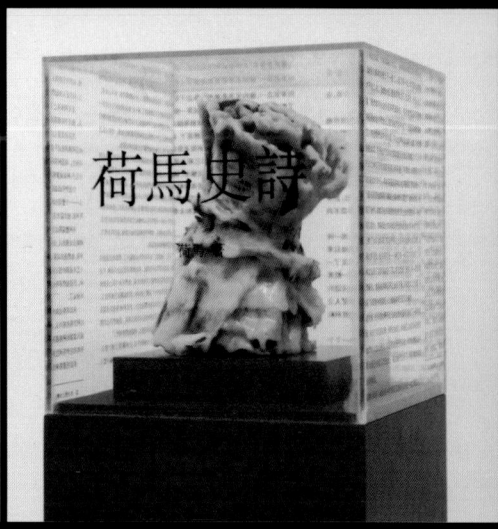
荷馬史詩

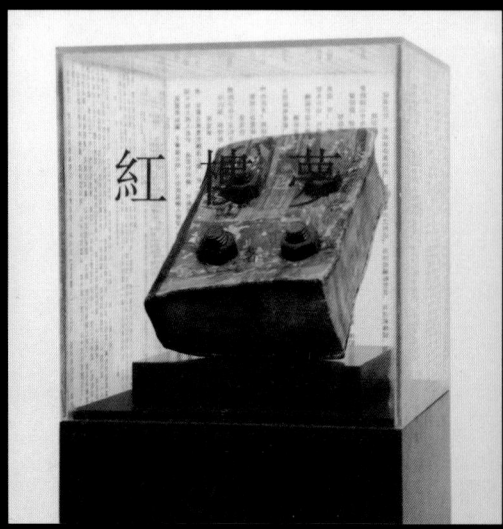
紅樓夢

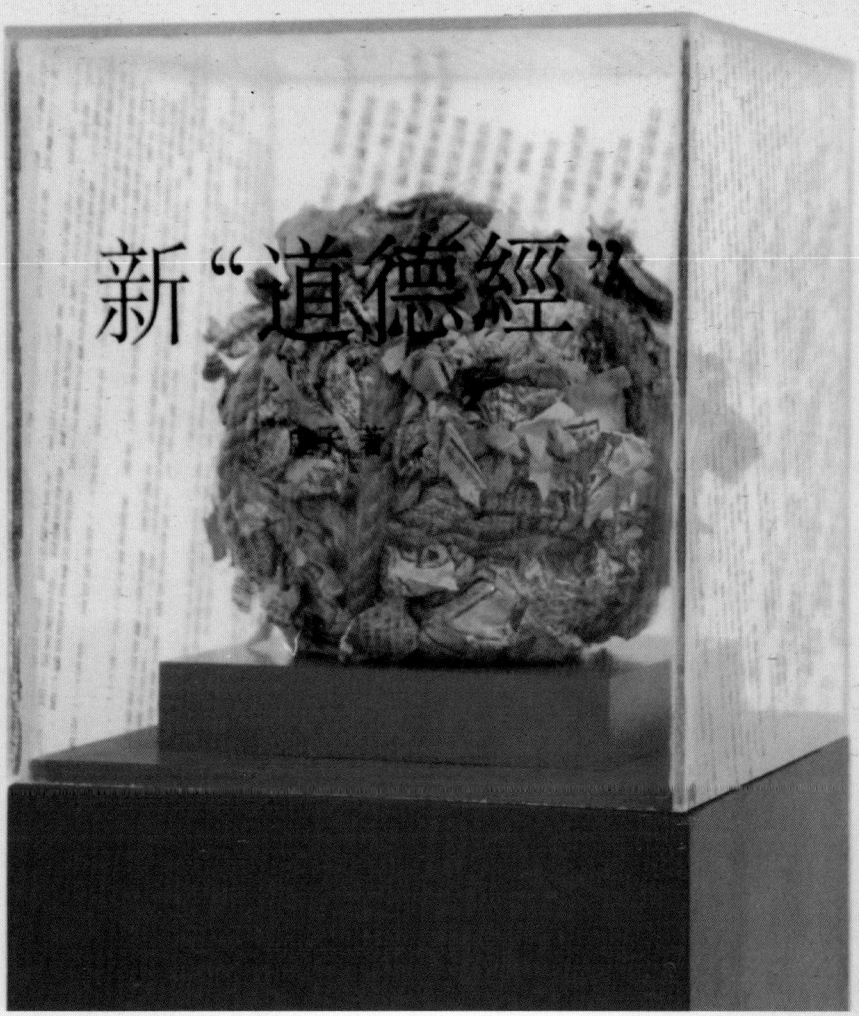
新“道德經”

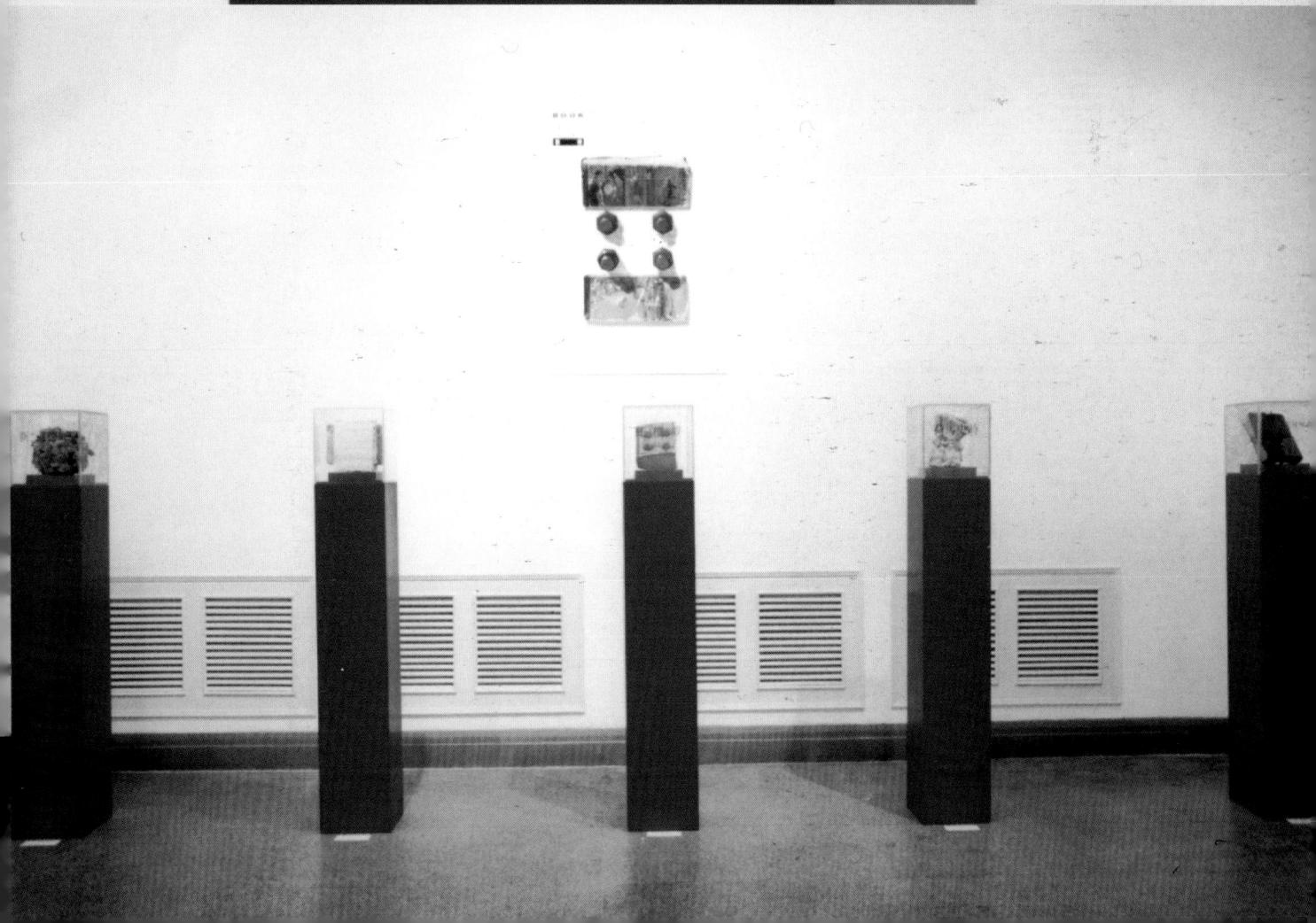

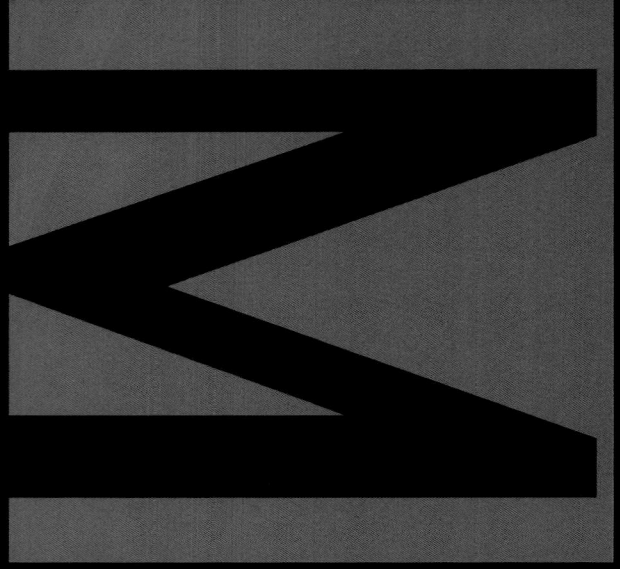

978 年出生于大连

1997 年考入中央美术学院设计系

2000 年获北京 2008 奥运会申办委员委会徽设计优秀奖

2000 年获香港刚古纸 VI 形象设计大赛北京区域奖

2001 年获靳埭强平面设计基金奖优异奖

2001 年招帖入选日本富山第六届国际招贴三年展

2001 年毕业于中央美术学院获学士学位

王雪皎

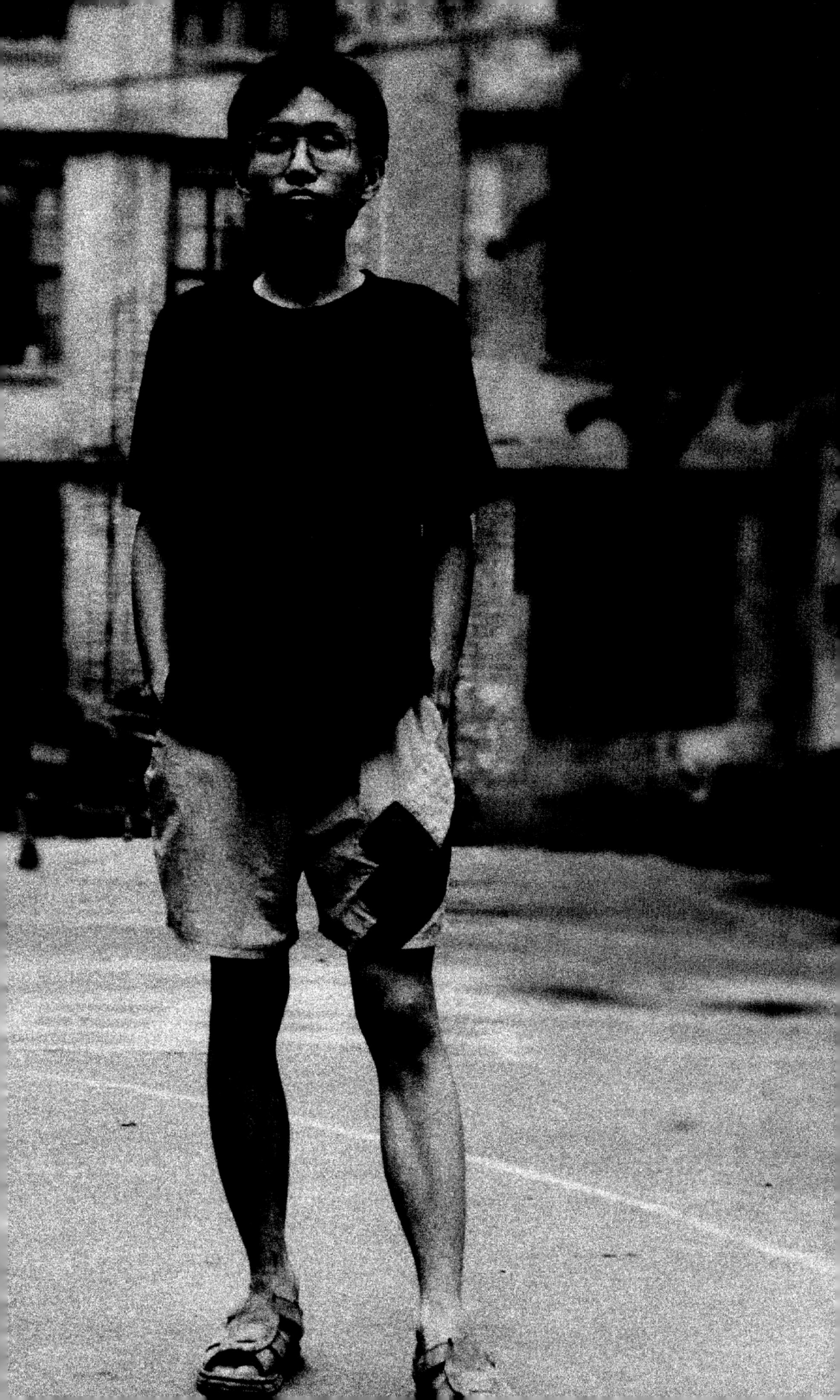

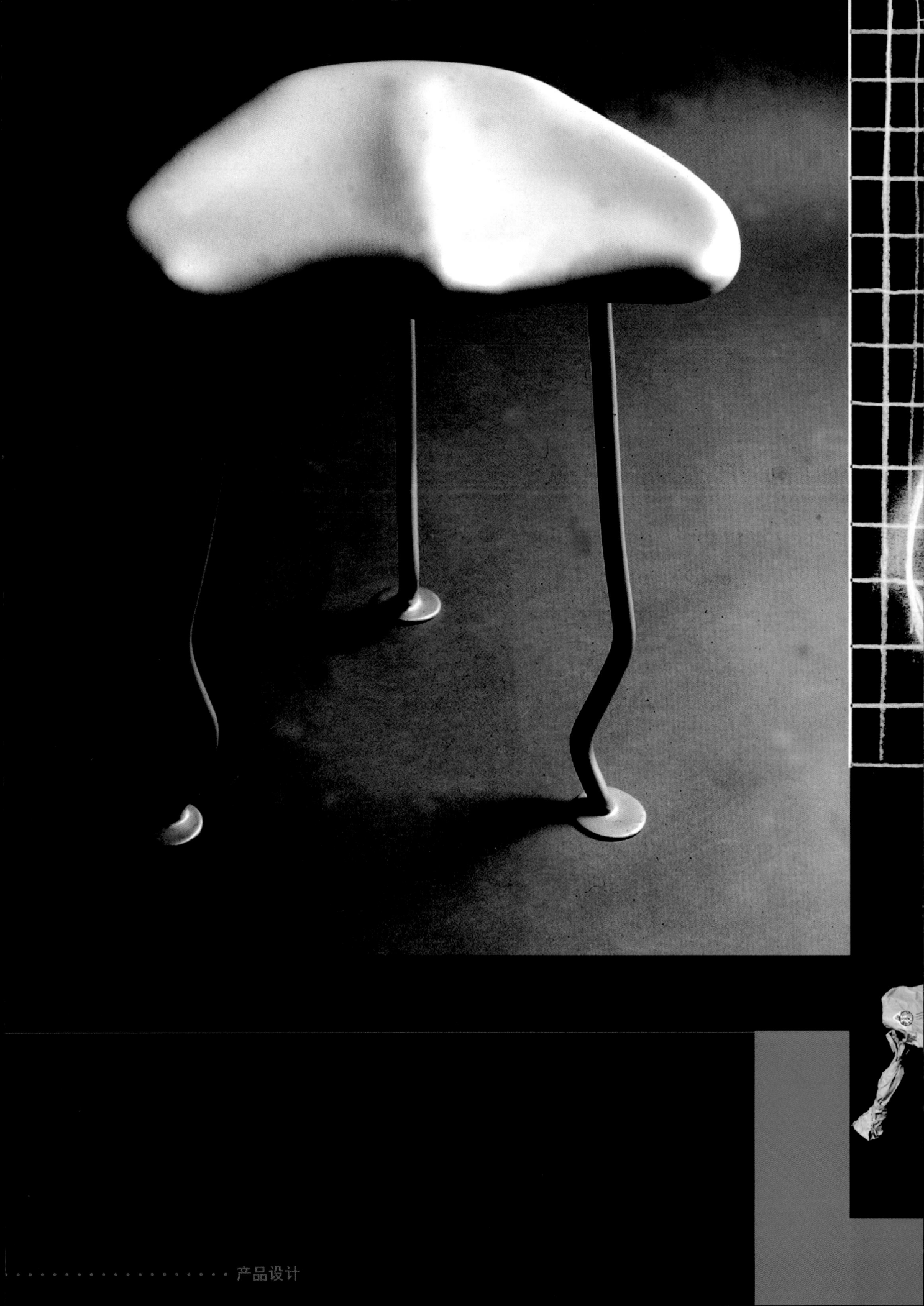

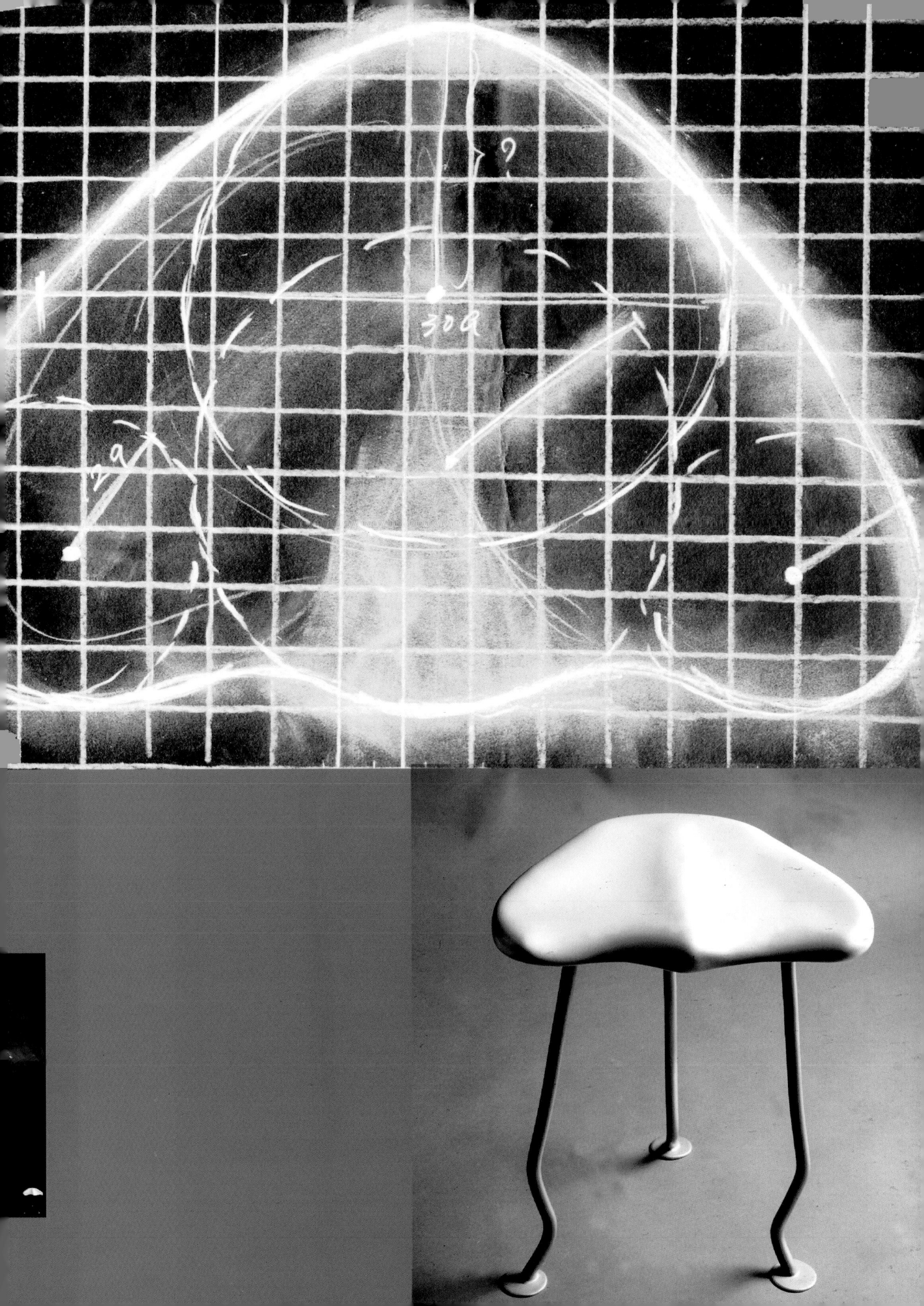

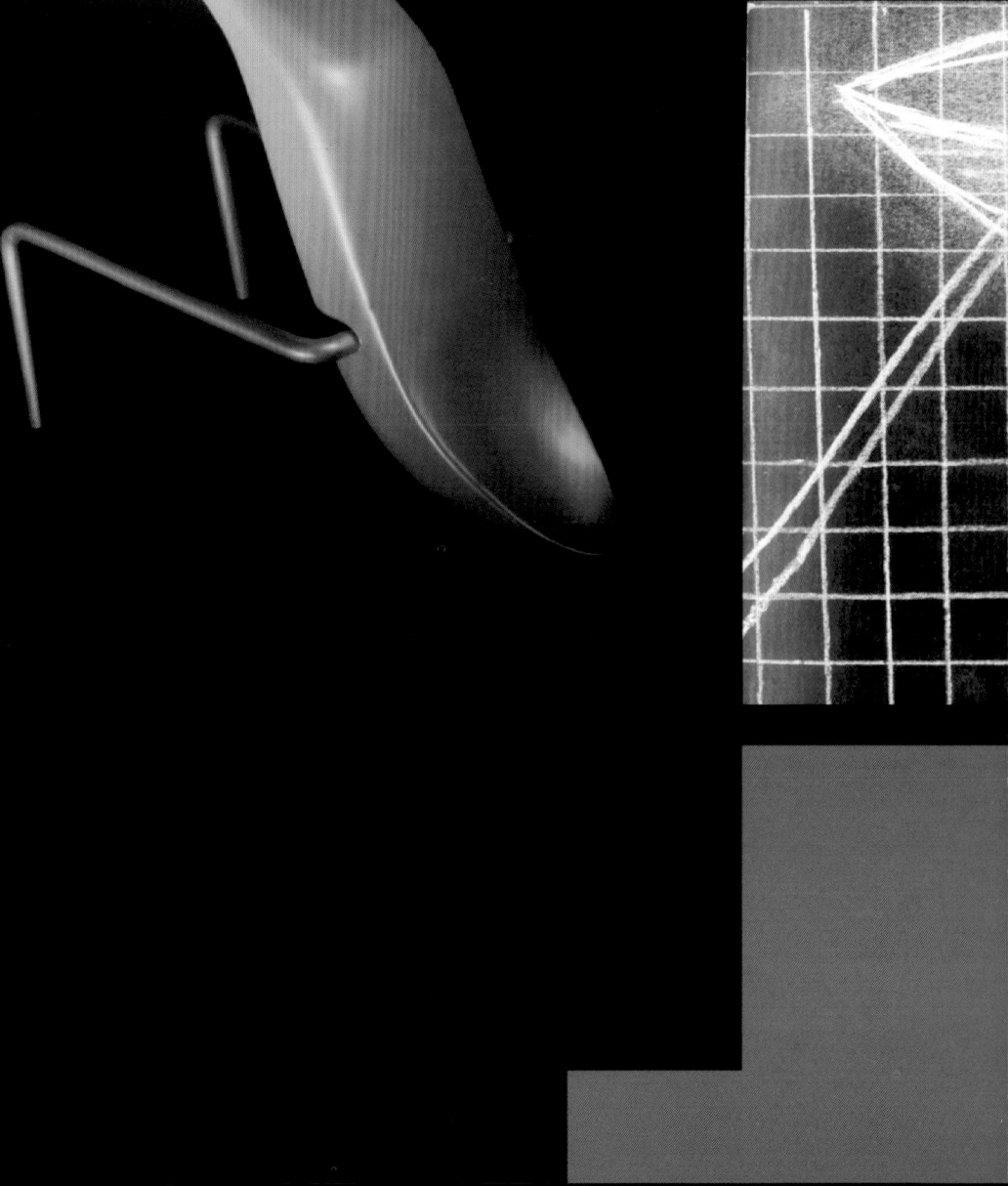

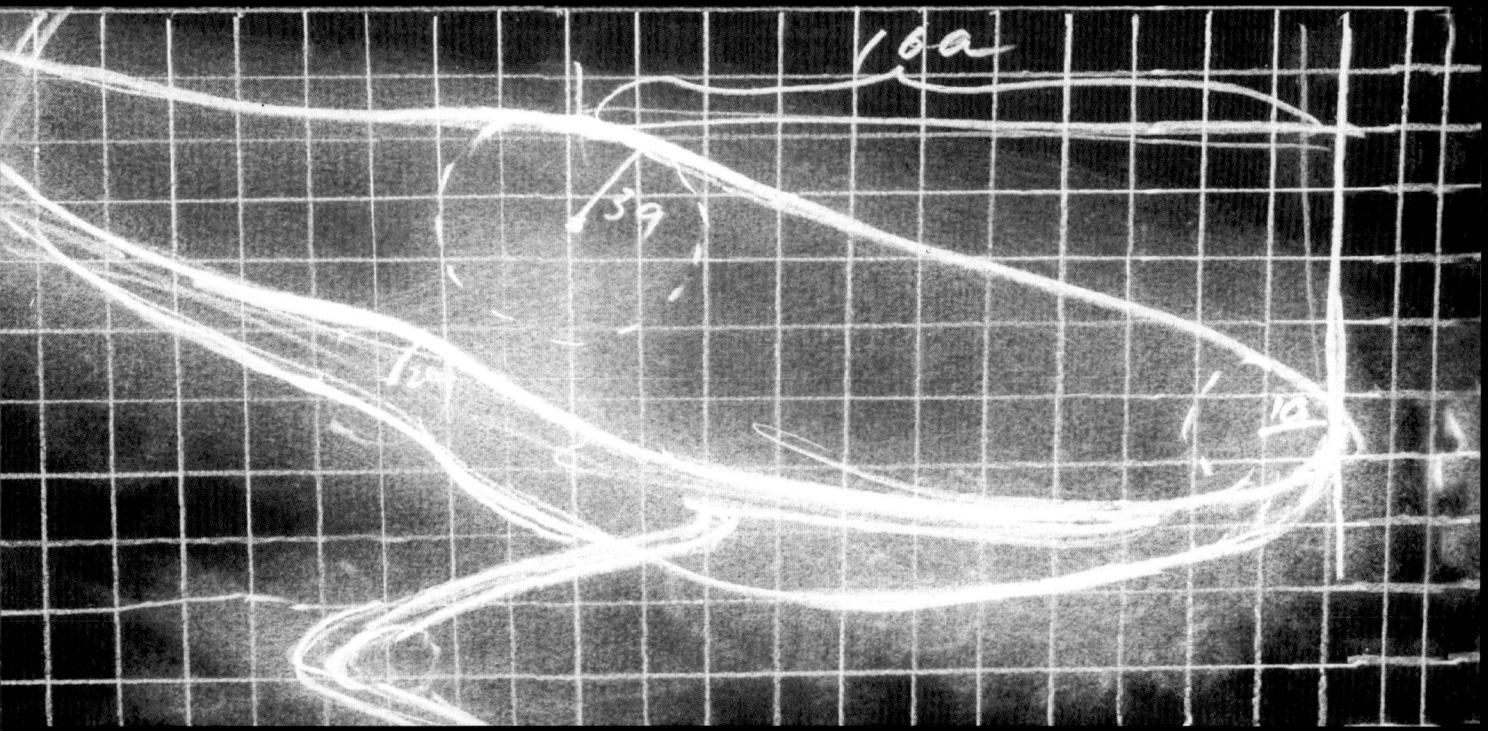
100
39
10

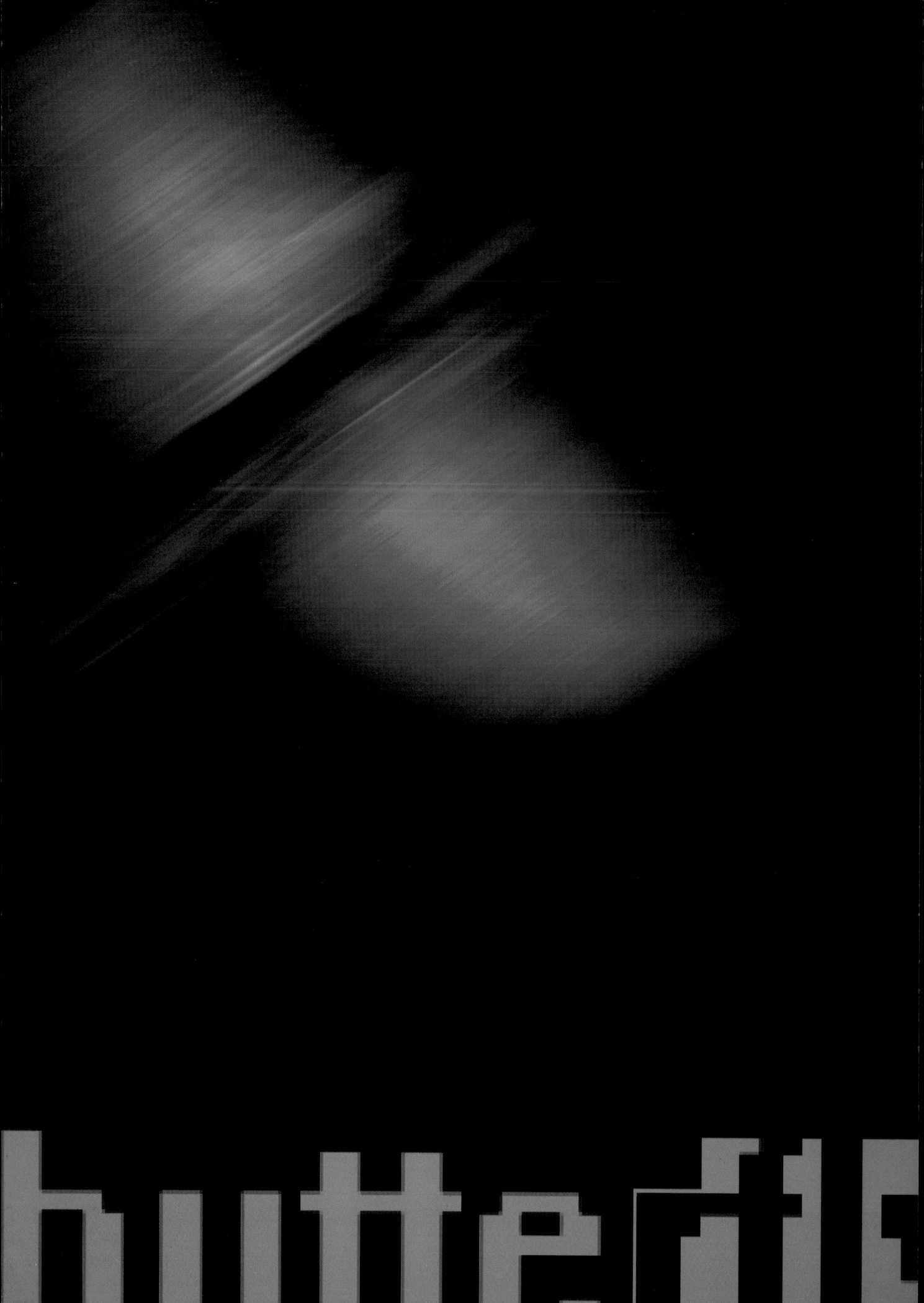
butterfl

一段物是人非的花样年华时光如昙花一现

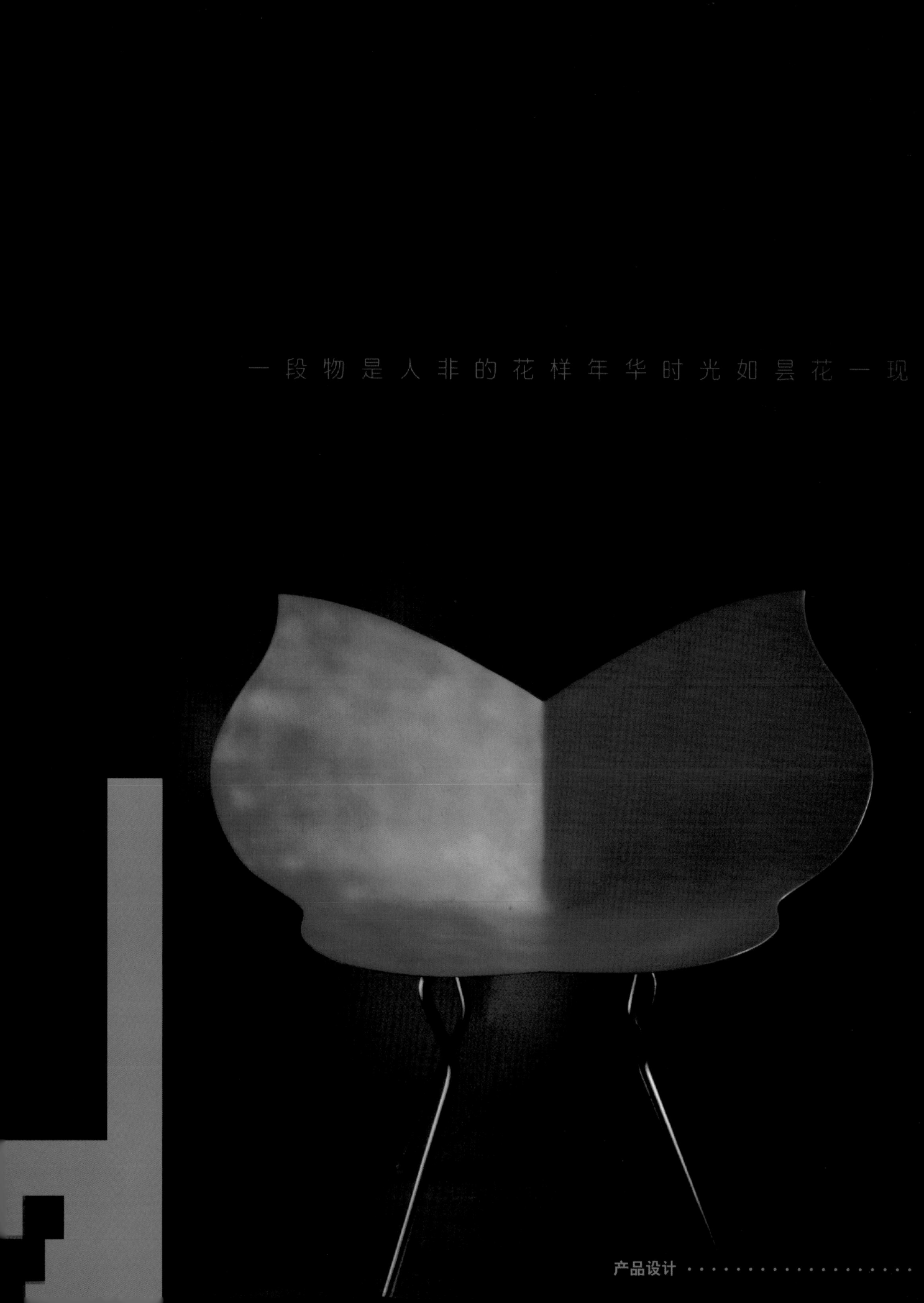

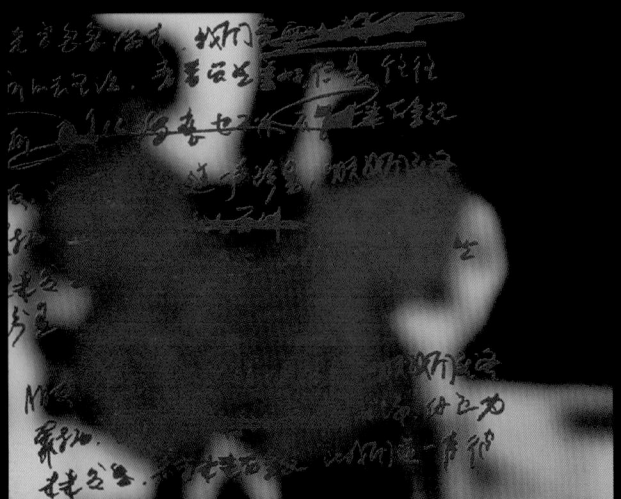

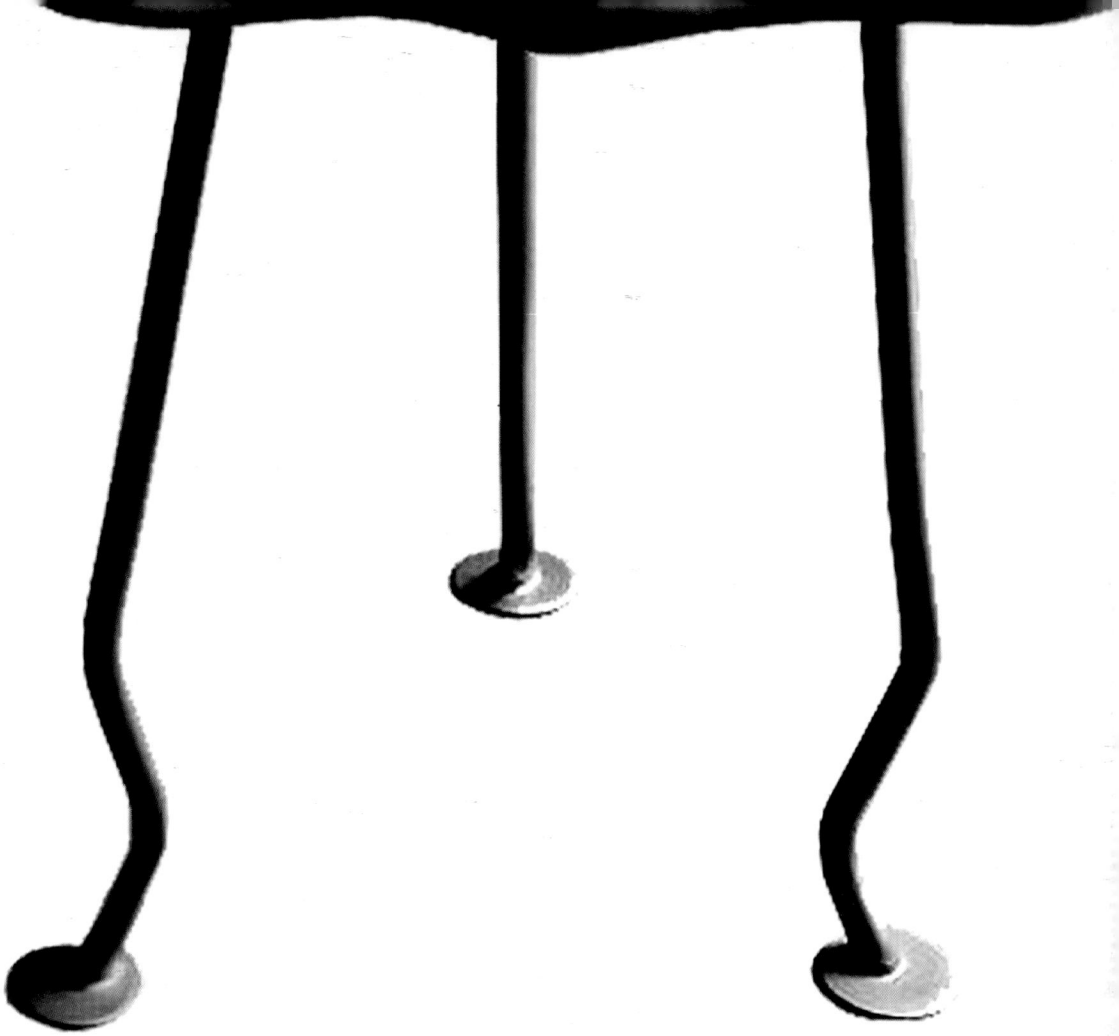

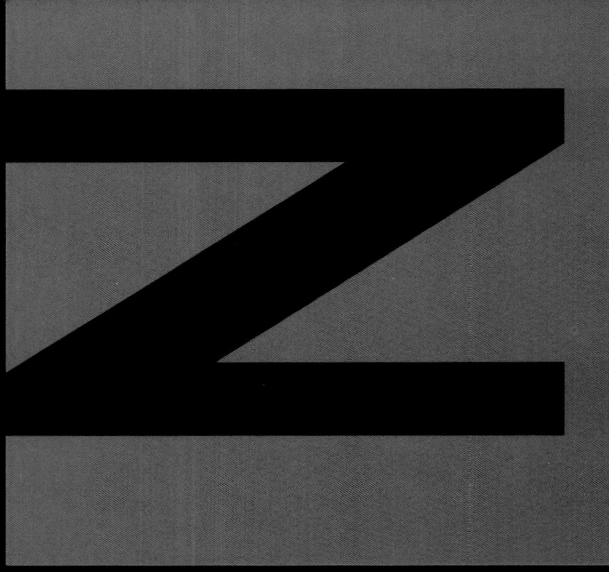

梁远苇

1977 年出生于北京

1995 年毕业于中国科技大学附中

1999 毕业于中央美术学院设计系获学士学位

2000 年就职于北京正邦文化艺术发展有限责任公司任艺术总监

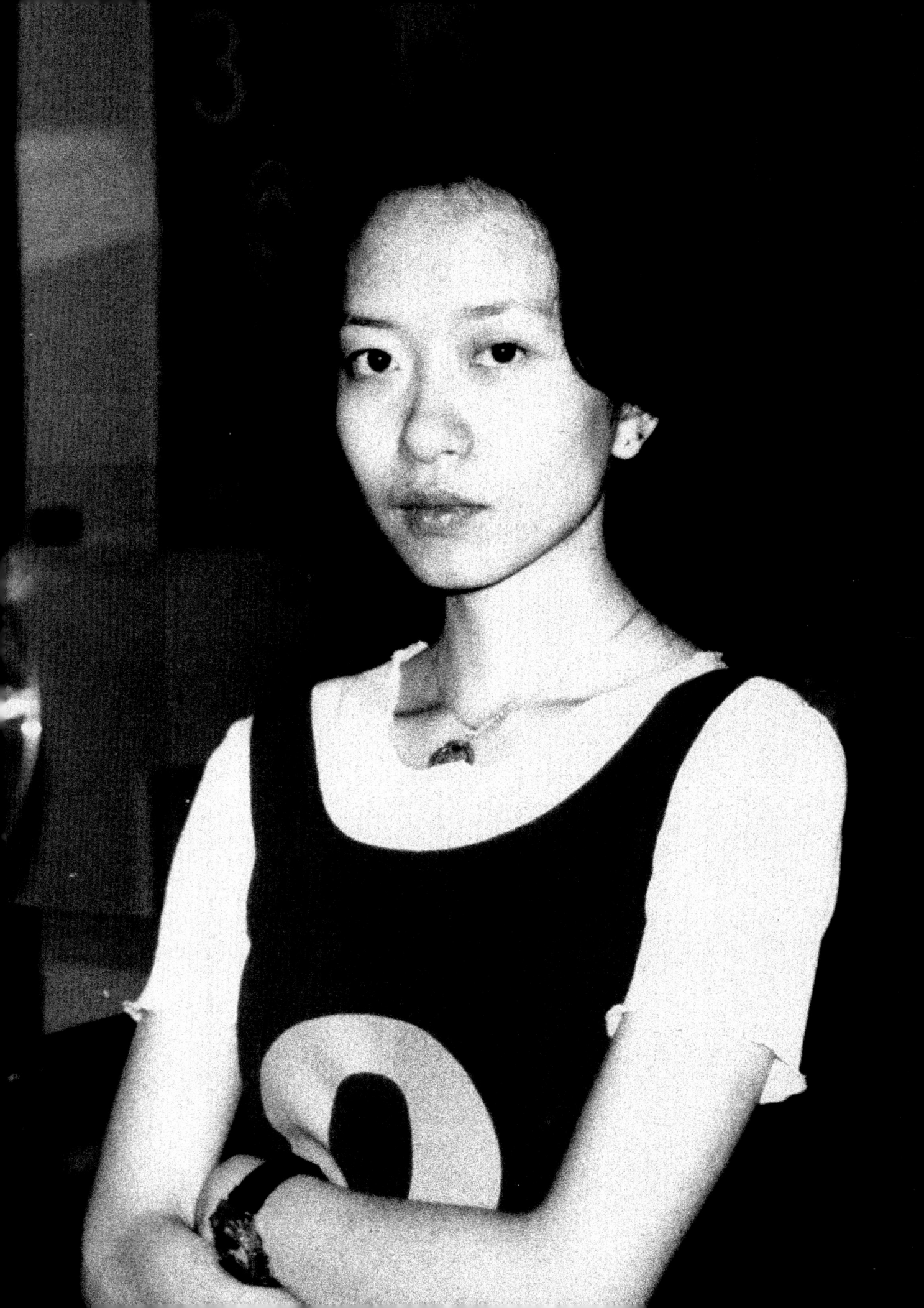

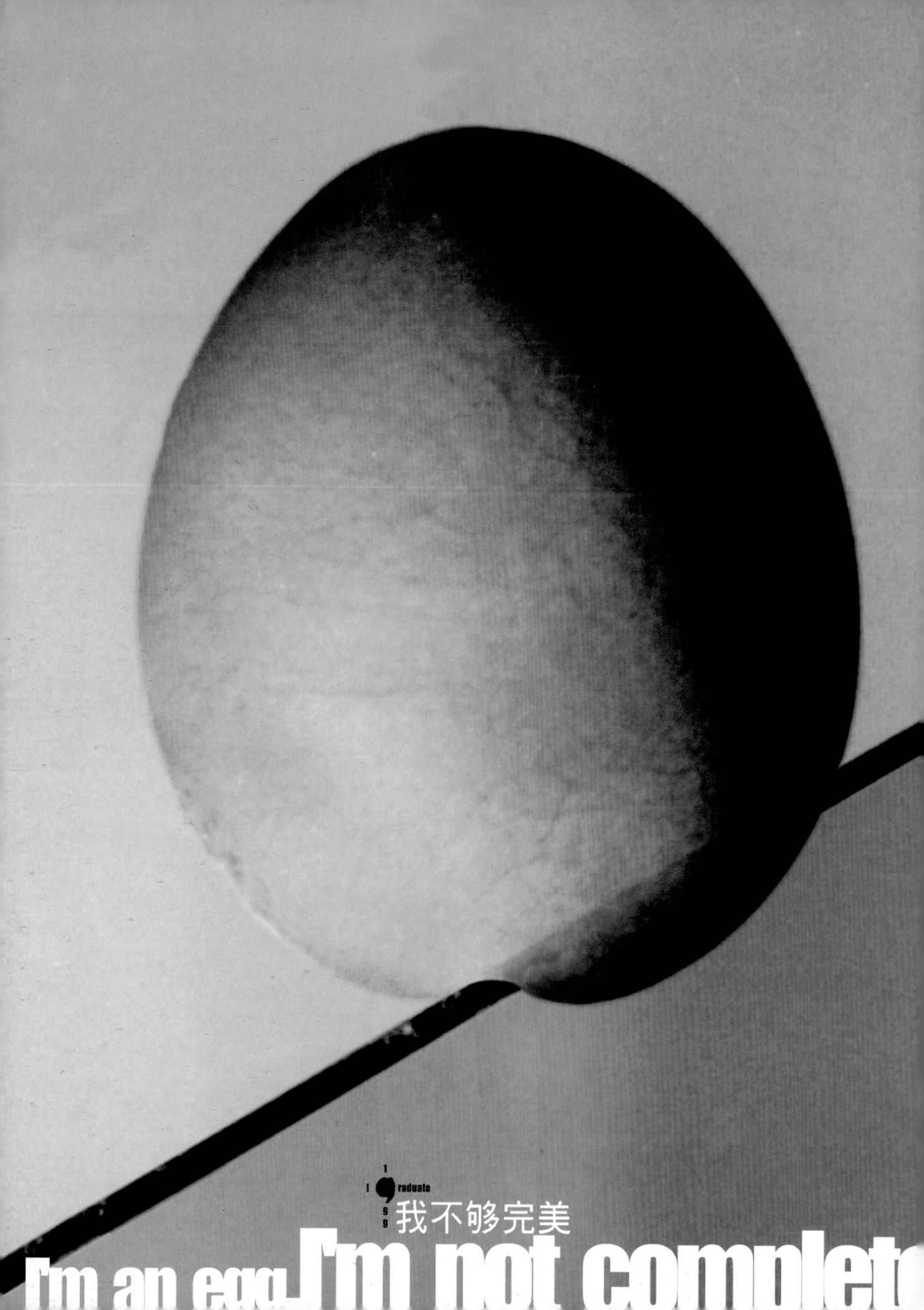
1
I raduate
9
9
我不够完美
I'm an egg
I'm not complete

我不够坚硬

I'm an egg, I'm not tough

我不够强壮

I'm an egg, I'm not tough

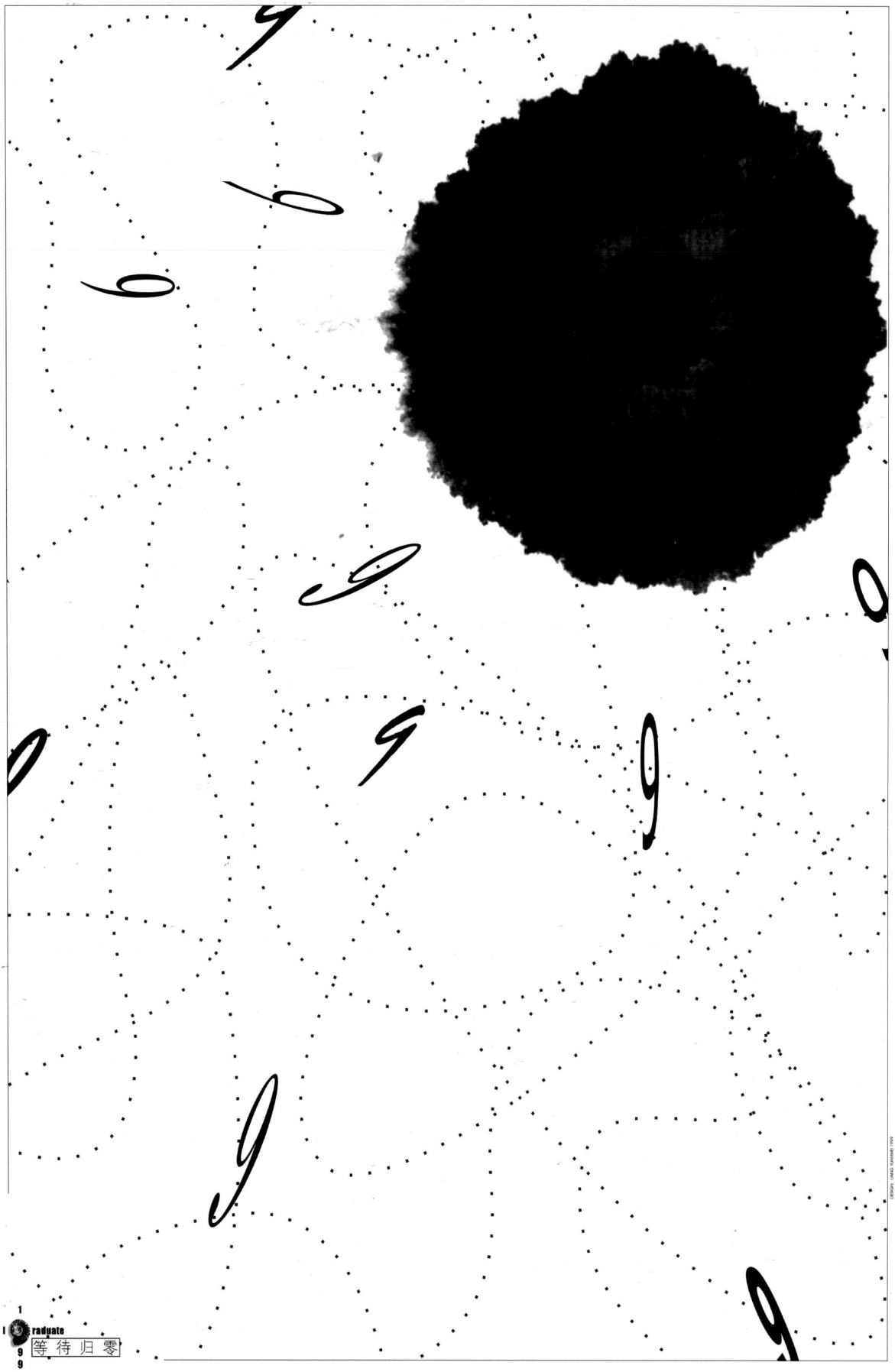

DESIGN: LIANG YONGMIN 1999

1999 Graduate

等待归零

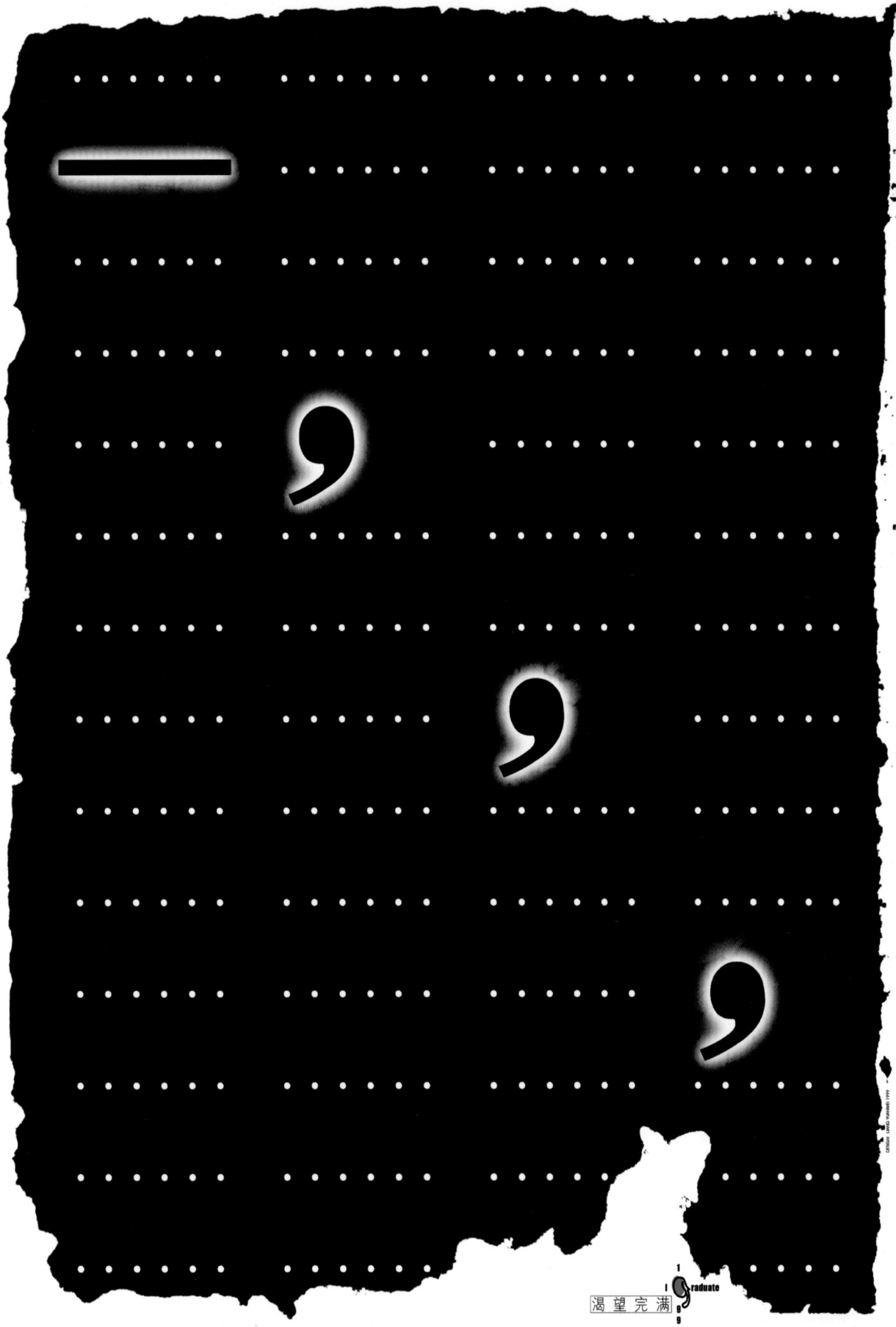
渴望完满
1999
Graduate

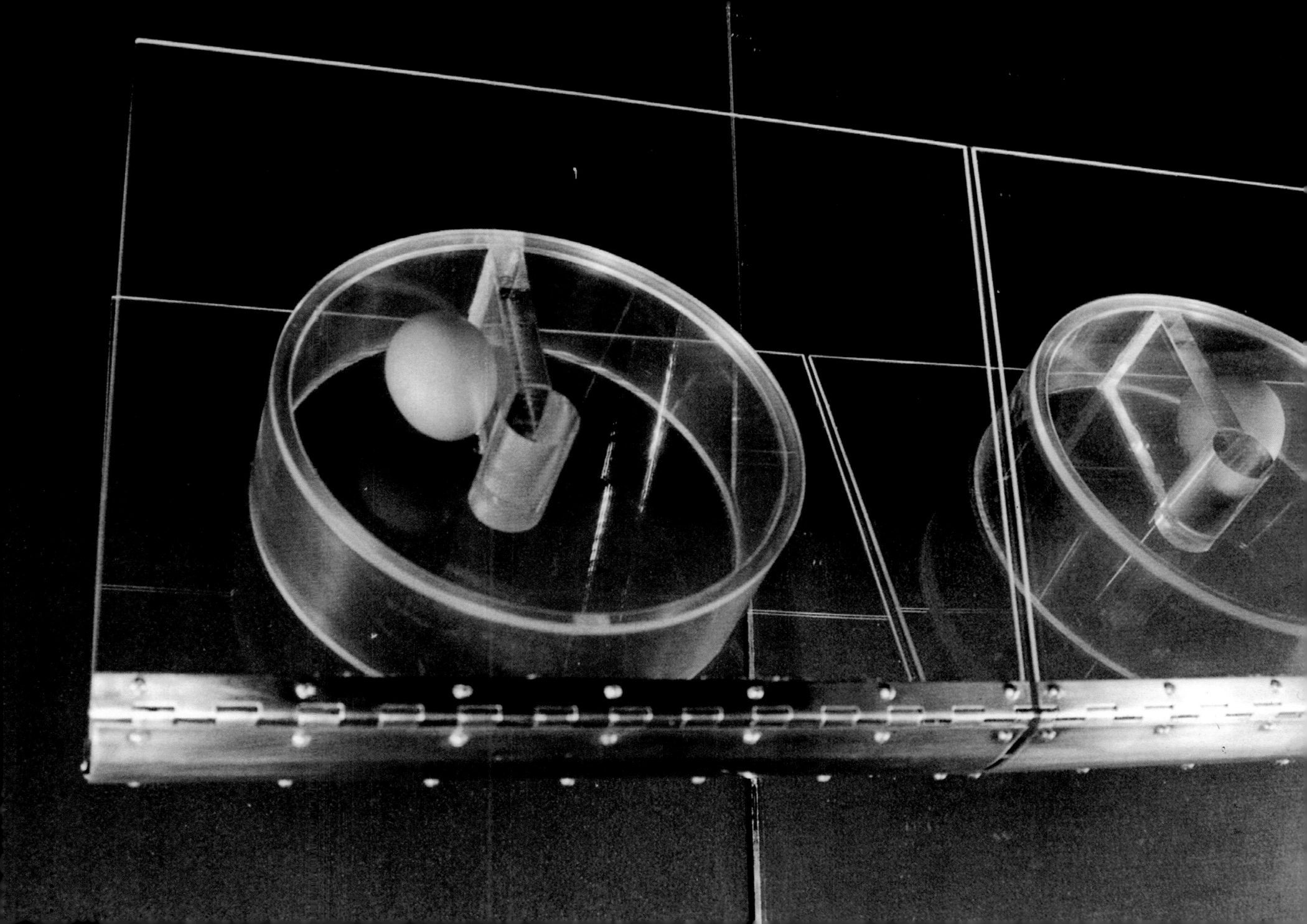

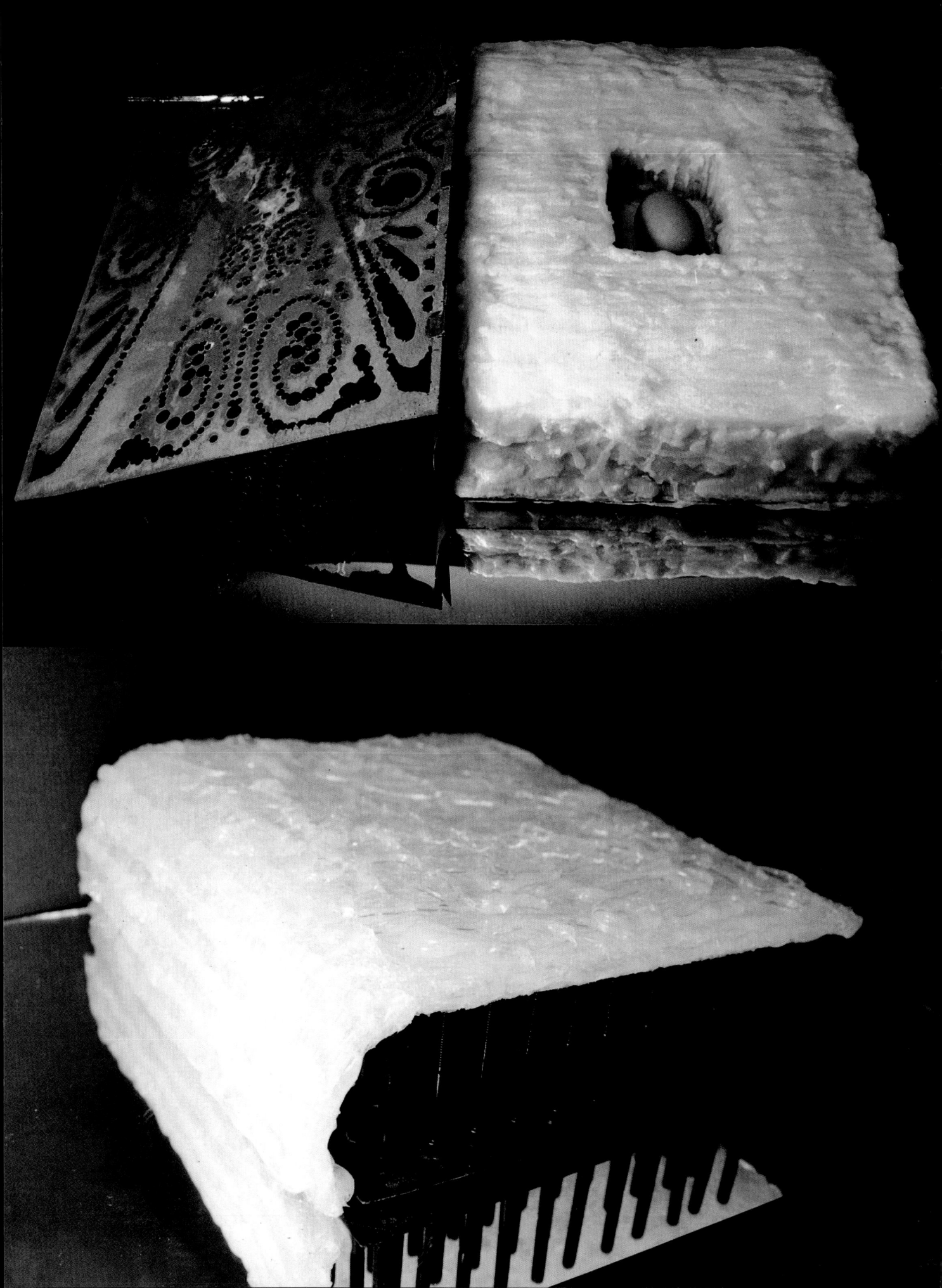

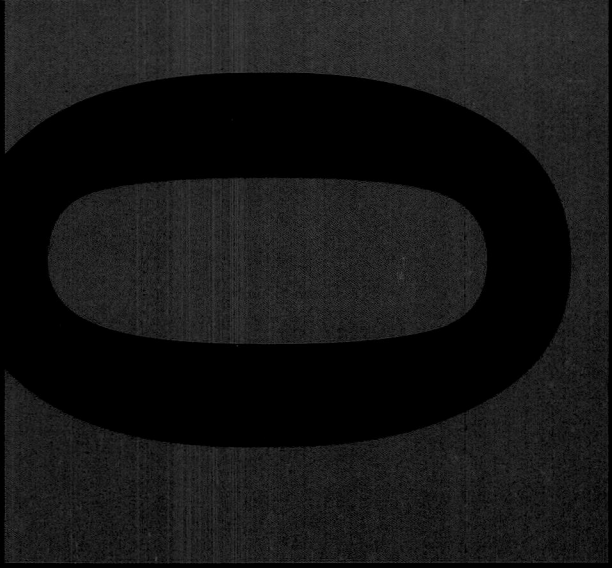

吴笛笛

1976 年出生于四川重庆

997 年考入中央美术学院设计系

2001 年毕业于中央美术学院获学士学位

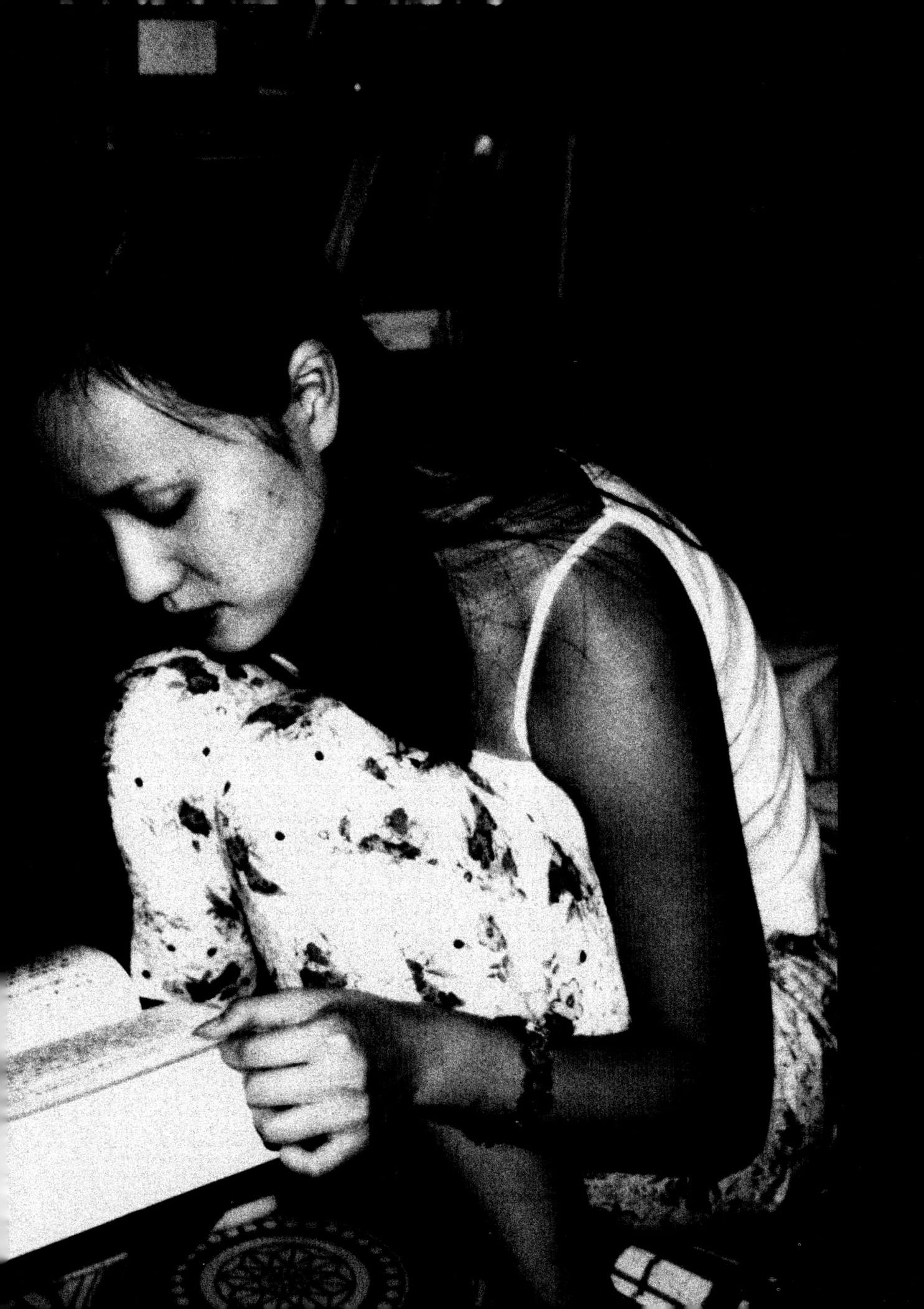

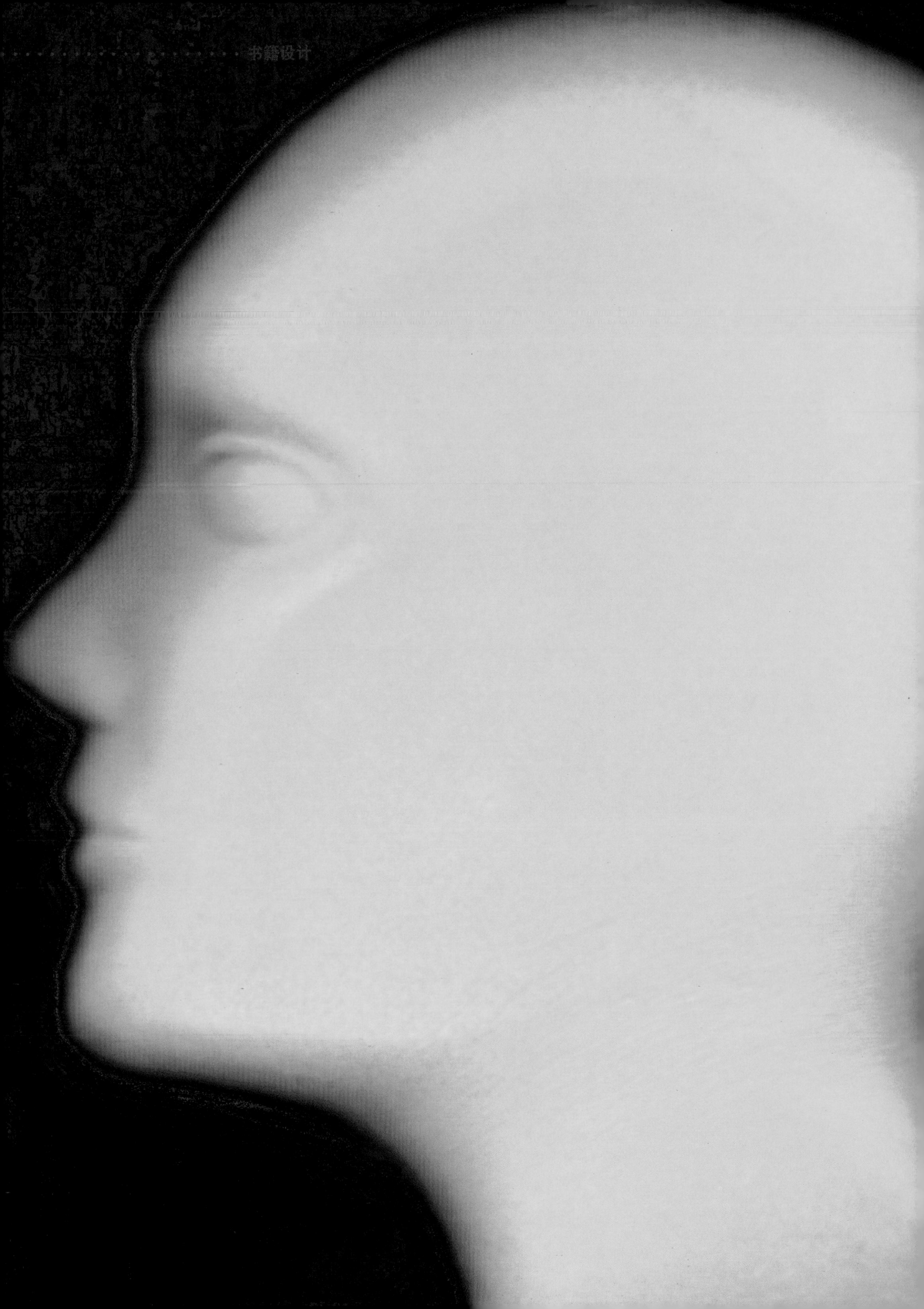

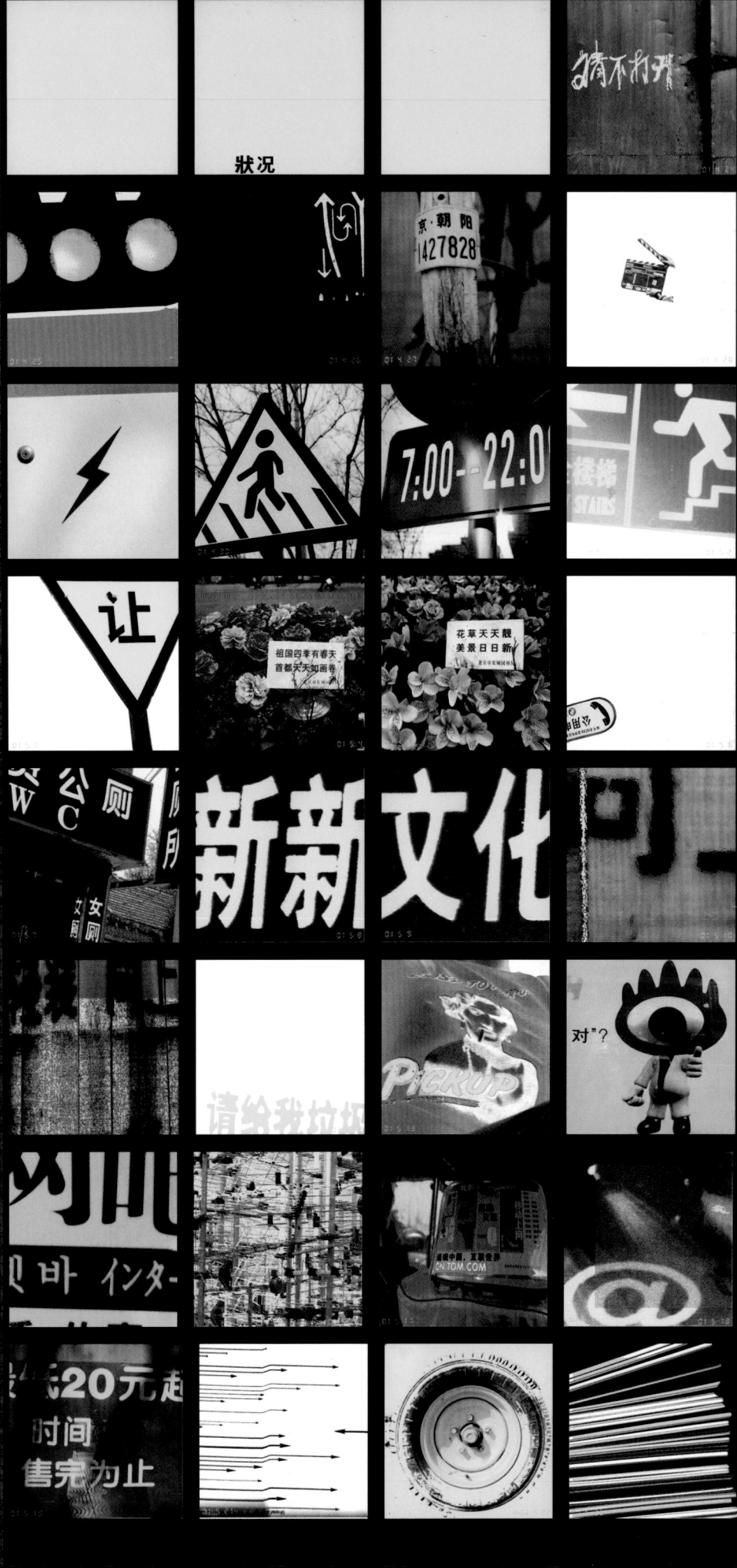
状况
京·朝阳
1427828
7:00--22:0
楼梯
STAIRS
让
祖国四季有春天
首都天天如画卷
花草天天靓
美景日日新
公厕
女厕
新新文化
PICKUP
对"?
CN.TOM.COM
时间
售完为止

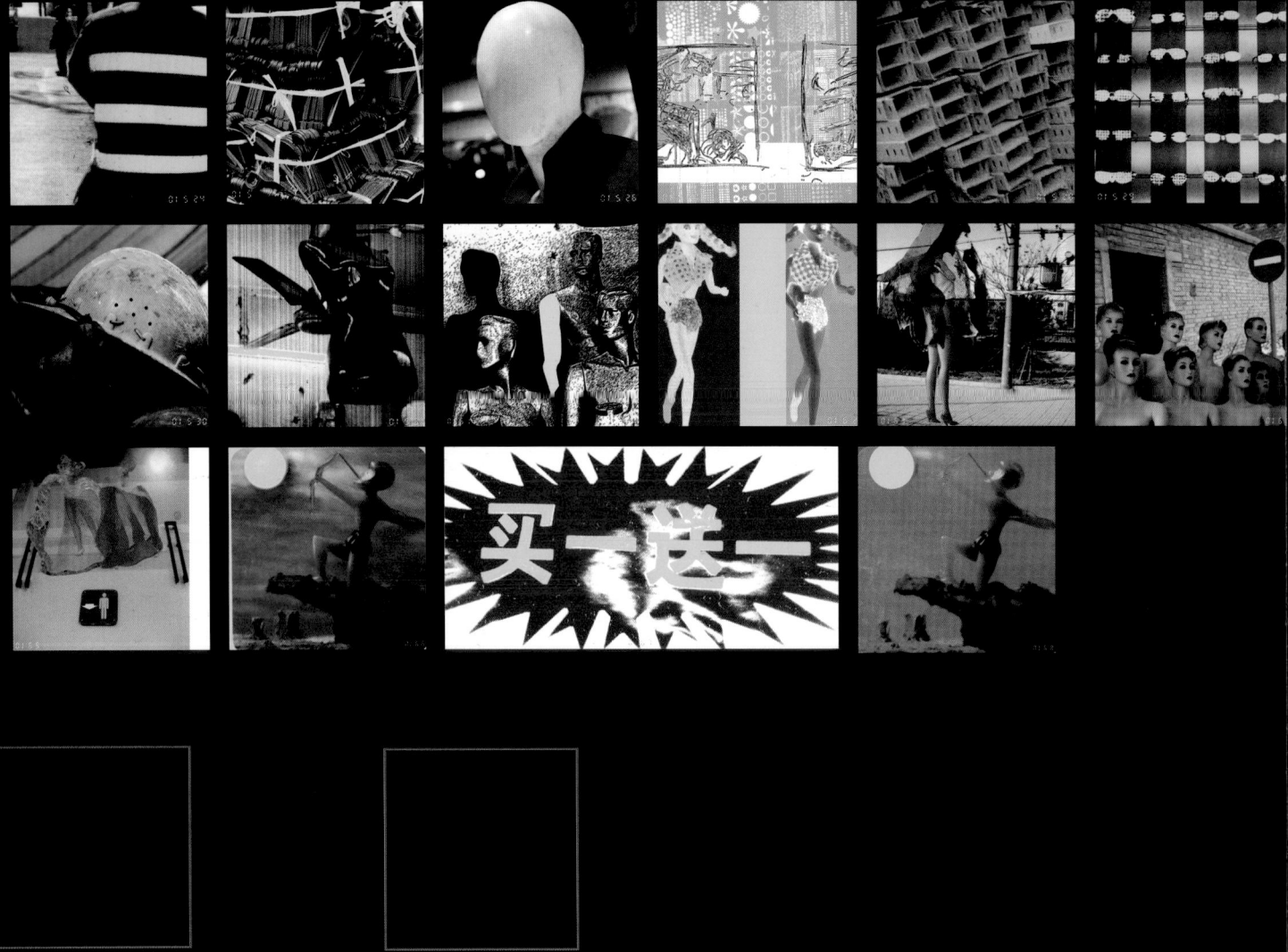
买一送一

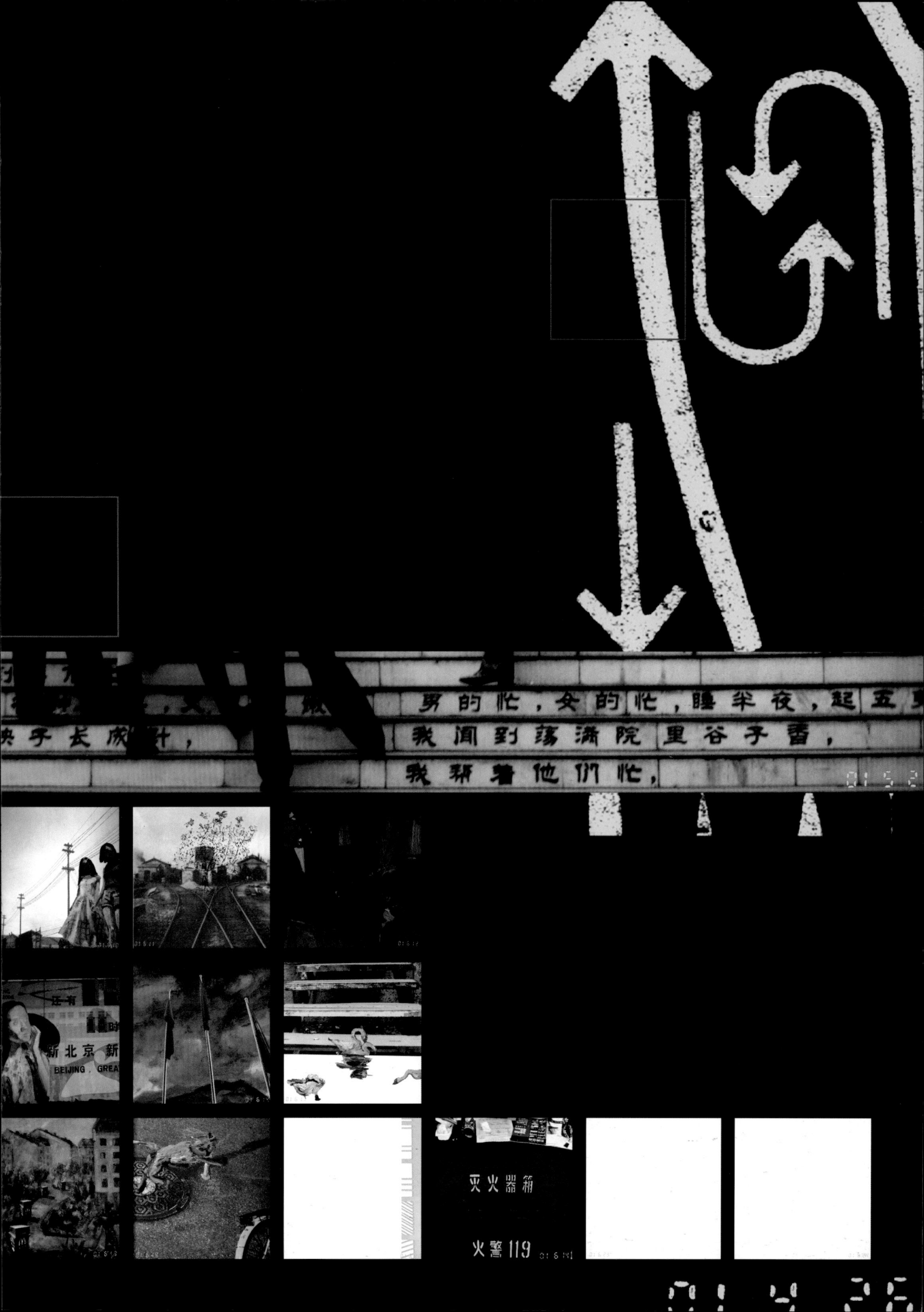
男的忙，女的忙，睡半夜，起五
我闻到荡满院里谷子香，
我瞧着他们忙，
还有
新北京 新
BEIJING, GREA
灭火器箱
火警119